THE UNPRIVATE LIFE
OF A
PASTOR'S WIFE

by

Frances Nordland

MOODY PRESS · CHICAGO

Library of Congress Catalog Card Number: 72-77945

ISBN: 0-8024-9042-5

Second Printing, 1974

Printed in the United States of America

Contents

1

The Unprivate Life of a Pastor's Wife

In 1969 the radio stations of the Moody Bible Institute included with their printed quarterly program schedule a questionnaire for listeners. The station managers hoped that answers to the questions would be helpful in planning future programming.

This notation that appeared on one questionnaire was given me: "I would like programs to help ministers' wives especially. There must be hundreds of us who listen, and at least 25 percent must be on the verge of nervous breakdowns."

The age bracket checked by this pastor's wife was 36 to 45 years of age, and she indicated that her family included children who were still in the home. She also noted that the station's programming met her needs most of the time.

The station manager commented in his letter to me, "I don't know if this woman's percentage is correct, but I think her statement is a rather startling one. As I think of several women I know who are in this category right now, it may not be too far off!"

Reading his comment, I recalled an article in *Time* in 1961 which dealt with the problem of breakdowns among ministers' wives.

You may be asking, "Why are the wives of ministers breaking down?" Perhaps you are wondering if the answer is the same as for the minister who breaks down: "Too much work at too many kinds of jobs."

I don't think that is the answer. Women in all ages have shown themselves to be able to take a lot of work. What a tremendous amount of strenuous work was done by pioneer women who worked alongside their husbands! Today, any mother of four or five small children has a pretty strenuous schedule, too, even though she has many servants (push-button appliances!). She is on call twenty-four hours a day, and she undertakes more activities than pioneer women did—like family chauffeuring, errands which take her to the supermarket, the dry cleaners, and so on. But if her attitude is positive, she can take it. However, if her attitude is negative for one reason or another, she may feel trapped and consequently experience psychological fatigue.

Breakdowns among ministers' wives—as well as among women who are not ministers' wives—are often due to inner conflict. In the case of the minister's wife the conflict may be between what her husband's congregation expects of her, what her husband expects of her, what she expects of herself because of an "image" she has of the ideal minister's wife, *and* what she actually wants to be and do. (When I use the phrase "ideal minister's wife" I don't mean the wife of an *ideal minister* but the *ideal wife* of a minister.)

Many a modern young woman who has married a minister says she wants fulfillment as a person, and she doesn't want to be pressed into a mold that she feels is out-of-date and unrealistic. On the other hand, some really want to live up to the picture of the ideal minister's wife, but they feel inadequate and are overcome by feelings of inferiority—and discouragement.

One woman from a suburb south of Chicago wrote, "Please pray for me. I would like to be the kind of mother and pastor's wife God intends for me to be, and as a young woman of 34 I'm encountering many obstacles. I feel the need to pray for encouragement, and I can't seem to pull up out of my discouragement. . . . As you pray for people everywhere, remember me."

Another wrote, "I'd appreciate very much your writing to me and giving me a few pointers to help me serve the Lord better as a pastor's wife."

A woman from a town in northwestern Illinois wrote, "As a young mother I need many words of wisdom. I have a boy two years old and a new little girl just four weeks old. I am also a pastor's wife. At times I get very discouraged with people, and have to commit my feelings to the Lord. . . . I am very inexperienced at entertaining and will need some help along this line. . . . Could you recommend any books for a young pastor's wife? I feel so unprepared for this position. I guess this is because it is a position where you are apt to be the object of criticism, and I want to be perfect."

One woman felt inadequate because, as she said, "I'm without the background of a Christian home."

A number of women have spoken about feeling inadequate for entertaining in their homes, and yet they feel this is an important facet of their role as hostess in the parsonage.

A woman in Florida wrote to me saying, "I am a pastor's wife. *You* understand, since you were a pastor's wife, how busy a person can be and at the same time how necessary it is to entertain. I like to have guests in our home, and my husband and I both believe in simplicity in entertaining. . . . Perhaps the worst *frustration* in entertaining is when well-meaning guests come and sit down in the kitchen to visit while I'm putting the last-minute touches on the meal. This is the hardest time to be civil, and to remember all the little details and whether I added salt to the vegetables. How do you handle these situations in a gracious manner?"

I suggested to my correspondent that perhaps her husband, knowing how she feels about having visitors in the kitchen

just before the meal, could suggest to a guest heading toward
the kitchen, "Why don't you stay in the living room and visit
until Ruth's ready? Since she can't concentrate on cooking
while carrying on a conversation, she might spoil the meal!
And that would make me one unhappy man!"

I anticipated that he might not want to cooperate in that
way, so I suggested that she might speak up and say something like this: "I'm one of those peculiar persons who have
a one-track mind. I just can't carry on a conversation while
I'm cooking without making a botch of the meal. So, in
deference to your stomach, please visit with my husband in
the living room!"

And I told her that if she feared a direct approach would
offend the woman, she might have a tray ready with crackers
prettily decorated with processed cheese from a pressurized
can, and ask her guest to fill glasses (ready on the tray) with
juice (tomato, apple, cranberry, or what have you?) and take
the tray to the living room to serve the guests before dinner.
This will keep the guests occupied while the hostess is taking
care of the last-minute details.

This problem presented by a minister's wife illustrates that
some of her problems are not much different from those of
other homemakers. Some are related especially to her role as
a pastor's wife, but I believe these would interest all churchwomen. For as they come to understand the inner conflicts
and tensions experienced by some pastors' wives, as well as
the joys and privileges and what is involved in their role, they
can be more sympathetic, understanding and cooperative. I
hope the churchwomen who read this book will be stimulated
to pray for their pastor's wife, for prayer is one way lay
people can help those who serve the Lord in the local church
ministry. The apostle Paul referred to such help when he
wrote, "I know that this shall turn to my salvation [which
could be translated deliverance, or preservation] through your

prayer, and the supply of the Spirit of Jesus Christ" (Phil 1:19).

Who can estimate what deliverances from burdens, from discouragement, from tensions and fears, will come to those for whom we fervently pray in the name of Jesus? If we faithfully pray for the pastor's wife, this influential person will be much more effective in her role.

My husband often says, "Behind every successful man, every good man, there is a good woman!" In other words, the woman behind the successful, good man is a VIP—a very important person.

I believe all women are VIPs because they are persons of influence. Every wife and mother has a great deal of influence; her primary influence is on her husband and children. But she also influences—though to a lesser extent—her neighbors, fellow church members, fellow workers at a place of employment, and those with whom she has social contacts.

But a minister's wife is a VIP in a special way because of her influence on the man to whom has been committed the spiritual leadership of a group of families who are associated in the worship and service of God in a local church and Sunday school. Her personal relationship with him as his wife affects him, as does her ability to meet the many demands made upon her as a mother, homemaker, and the wife of a minister.

I didn't really understand fully how much a wife can mean to a man who is a pastor until about a week before my first husband, Cornelius Beerthuis, died. At that time he expressed to me the thoughts that were in his heart about the church where he had most recently served, about our sons and their wives, our grandchildren, and me. Telling of his love for me, he added, "You have been such a wonderful helpmeet—in a thousand ways! I can't begin to tell you what you have meant to me during all these years. You have helped me so much. You have encouraged me so much. You stood by my side, and never failed me. I don't know how to express it, but I know that your love and devotion have been unfailing. I thank you for it."

You may wonder how I can remember the exact words. That day as I was sitting in his hospital room I was reading a book, *The Mystery of Suffering* by Hugh Evan Hopkins, and I had in my hand a pencil for underlining passages that especially spoke to my heart and for making notes. When he began talking to me, after his brothers and sisters from Grand Rapids, Michigan, had left, I realized that he had carefully thought out what he wanted to say to me in view of his feeling that the Lord would soon take him to heaven. I turned to the back of the book where there were some blank pages, and I wrote down what he said in shorthand. Later I typed copies for myself and for our sons because I wanted them to know that the one request he had made for his "dear sons and grandsons" was that they "grow up to be good, strong, stalwart Christians, living for Jesus every day."

If you are a pastor's wife, please don't underrate your influence on your husband.

If you are a churchwoman, please be compassionate as you think of your pastor's wife. Instead of criticizing her, pray for her, and be alert for ways to help her and to show kindness. Think of yourself as her prayer helper. I'm quite sure that the familiar phrase "prayer helper" comes from some words in 2 Corinthians 1:11—words which the apostle Paul wrote to the Christians at Corinth. Describing various trials and opposition he had experienced, he also spoke of deliverances, and then he referred to how *they* had helped him: "Ye also helping together by prayer for us." As you pray for your minister's wife, and she is strengthened and encouraged, and makes progress in her own spiritual growth, you will be helping your preacher's ministry.

THE PREACHER'S WIFE

There is one person in your church
　Who knows your preacher's life!
She's wept and smiled and prayed with him,
　And that's your preacher's wife!

She knows your prophet's weakest point
　And knows his greatest power;
She's heard him speak in trumpet tone
　In his great triumph hour.

She's heard him groaning in his soul
　When bitter raged the strife,
As, hand in his, she knelt with him—
　For she's the preacher's wife!

The crowd has seen him in his strength,
　When glistened his drawn sword;
As underneath God's banner folds,
　He faced the devil's horde.

But she knows deep within her heart
　That scarce an hour before,
She helped him pray the glory down
　Behind a fast closed door.

You tell your tales of prophets brave
　Who walked across the world
And changed the course of history
　By burning words they hurled.

And I will tell how, back of them,
　Some women lived their lives;
Who wept with them and prayed with them—
　They were the preachers' wives!

What about the mother I mentioned who had two young children and felt unprepared for her role as the wife of a minister "because it is a position where you are apt to be the object of criticism, and I want to be perfect"?

She might as well face this fact: she will never be perfect, and she will never be able to fulfill the expectations of everyone in their church.

Someone, sensing how impossible it is for the wife of a pastor to please everybody, listed desirable qualities for a minister's wife in a "Blueprint for the Ideal Preacher's Wife." A drawing of this composite creature showed her with four arms—to keep a neat, clean house at all times, to keep her family neat, clean and well dressed, to do all church work required, and to raise children to be intelligent and obedient. The hairdo on one side of her head differed in styling from the other side. The reason: "Hair—half in fashion of the day, other half in a motherly style." The front view of this woman showed only one eye in front—for playing the piano. A note indicated that she had one eye in back—to see what her children were doing in the front pew. She had an ear with an automatic sifter to sort out information which could be repeated from that which was to be kept confidential. Her mouth was described as "always smiling, saying good things." Her feet: "substantial—to work and work and work." Her figure: "not too glamorous and not too matronly." Body: "tireless." Clothing: "always neat, not too new, not too old, not too fancy, not too plain."

What kind of mind was she expected to have? Several descriptions were given: "Radar mind—to know exactly where to reach husband at all times. Automatic mind—to produce Sunday school lessons, youth lessons, assorted ladies' group devotions, parties, socials, and clever ideas to keep up husband's morale. File-cabinet mind, containing (1) miscellaneous file of all information that husband is apt to forget, (2) recipe file of 999 ways to prepare hamburger, (3) information on child psychology, marriage problems, and so on."

And to top everything off, this composite woman had an escape valve on top of her head—to relieve tensions.

And then an asterisk refers the reader of this blueprint

for the ideal preacher's wife to a note giving this information: "Available only with ideal preacher. We do not break a set!"

Humor can be a forceful means of communication, and it may be that some who have read that blueprint have come to the conclusion, "Well, I guess we have been expecting too much of the wife of our preacher."

A few years ago I came across a similar item, a "classified advertisement" prepared by Robert M. Boltwood, who was head of the technical writing division of Chevrolet Engineering Center, General Motors, and a teacher at Wayne State and Michigan State universities: "Applicant's wife must be both stunning and plain, smartly attired but conservative in appearance, gracious and able to get along with everyone, even women. Must be willing to work in church kitchen, teach Sunday school, baby-sit, run multilith machine, wait table, never listen to gossip, never become discouraged."

When you are tempted to be resentful because you think people in the church expect too much of you, a good attitude to take is this: "I am in this place because God has set me here, and He will make me adequate for filling this place in a way that will please Him."

Be sure of this: You will not be able to please everyone in the congregation, and you won't find peace of mind in trying to do so. But you will find peace of mind as you seek to please the Lord, and you will find that He will make you adequate for what He wants you to be and do.

I am confident of this, for I have experienced what the apostle Paul experienced, as stated in 2 Corinthians 3:5, "Our sufficiency is of God."

2

Be Realistic About Your Role

Where have ministers' wives and church people gotten their concept of what the minister's wife ought to be? From the Bible?

You don't get much of a picture of her role from the Bible, for only a few references are made to women who could be classed as ministers' wives. The apostle Peter's wife might be cited. We know Peter was married because the gospels contain the account of Jesus healing Peter's mother-in-law. Also, the apostle Paul refers to Cephas (another name for Peter) as one who availed himself of the privilege to "lead about . . . a wife" (1 Co 9:5).

Paul wrote to the young pastor Timothy that the bishop (or overseer or minister) was to be "the husband of one wife" (1 Ti 3:2). In that section of Scripture no qualifications are given for the wife of a minister, but it says the wives of deacons were to "be grave, not slanderers, sober, faithful in all things" (v. 11).

We need to recognize that in the early church period the leaders of the church were men whom we would now designate as laymen. There was no separation, as now, between clergy and laymen, making a separate class of people in the church known professionally as "ministers." So, if you want to learn from the Bible what a minister's wife should be like, you must look for references to wives. You will find no double standard—one for the pastor's wife and one for the layman's wife.

14

Next, remember that most of the life pictured in the Bible was agrarian. Men were, for the most part, farmers and shepherds. The life of the wife was taken up with domestic duties, and her primary sense of fulfillment came through the work she did in her home—spinning, weaving, bringing up her children, and caring for the needs of her husband. This is the kind of woman described in Proverbs 31, though you must admit she was quite a business woman. She bought and sold property, she purchased raw material from merchants for the small manufacturing business in her home (weaving), and she sold her finished products to the merchants. All this was in addition to her work of managing the household which consisted of numerous maidens who assisted her.

This woman's rewards, as depicted in Proverbs 31, included seeing her husband honored in the community, seeing her children grow up as godly men and women, seeing them marry and have children. In all this, her influence had been important. Her relationship to her husband was that of a helpmeet for him. Her husband was head of the house.

Woman's status was elevated through Christianity, yet her main work was in the home. In his epistle to Titus, Paul gave instructions about the conduct of the older women. They, with behavior "as becometh holiness," were to "teach the young women to be sober, to love their husbands, to love their children, to be discreet, chaste, keepers at home, good, obedient to their own husbands, that the word of God be not blasphemed" (2:3-5).

Though early church leaders were married, it wasn't long before voices began to be raised calling for a celibate clergy, and this was the general practice until the Protestant Reformation. Martin Luther, after the severance of his connection with the established church, hadn't intended to marry. When he first learned that some nuns and monks had left convents and monasteries to marry, he exclaimed: "Good heavens!

They won't give *me* a wife." But he did marry when he was forty-two.

Kathy Von Bora, whom Luther married, was one of twelve nuns whose departure from a convent had been arranged by Luther. After more than a year, all had married except three, and Kathy was one of them. Finally, when only she remained single, she half jokingly proposed marriage to Luther. He wasn't interested. When he mentioned the incident to his father, he took it quite seriously and urged Martin to marry Kathy, who was then in her late twenties. Martin often called Kathy "his rib," a reference to Genesis 2, where we read that "the LORD God caused a deep sleep to fall upon Adam." While he slept, God "took one of his ribs, and closed up the flesh instead thereof; and the rib, which the Lord God had taken from man, made he a woman, and brought her unto the man." Adam said, "This is now bone of my bones, and flesh of my flesh: she shall be called Woman, because she was taken out of Man."

Kathy Von Bora Luther, the first Protestant minister's wife, was deeply devoted to her husband. Since many guests came to their home to talk to this renowned man, Kathy's role was that of a hostess and, according to the customs of the times, she would be on the fringe of the conversational circle. Apparently she did not resent being in the background.

At a meeting for ministers' wives to whom I had been invited to speak a few years ago, I addressed them as a privileged group of women, and then asked this rhetorical question: "Do you realize that in England a little over 350 years ago a group similar to this one would be an illegal group?"

Not until 1604 did the matter of a married clergy become a settled issue in England. Prior to this it was illegal for a minister to have a wife, although some did. One of these was Thomas Cranmer, who lived from 1489 to 1556, and was the first Protestant Archbishop of Canterbury. It is recorded that his wife lived in such retirement that when she traveled she made the journey in a box with a ventilating lid.

Anyone making a historical survey of ministers' wives would be confronted with this question: What about their history in frontier America? Information about the clergyman's wife during that period is limited. Someone has said that these women, like their preacher-husbands, were too busy making history to spend much time recording their deeds.

What about the minister's wife today? Much more has been written about her in the twentieth century than in previous periods of history, and this has contributed to the image that the minister's wife of today has of herself.

The December, 1961, issue of *Pastoral Psychology,* devoted entirely to the subject of the minister's wife, was described as having "been in the making for three years. Most of the articles are based on research, which is a rarity for literature concerning the pastor's wife. The preponderance of what has been previously written has been done by wives themselves, based primarily on individual personal experience."[1]

Wallace Denton in his book, *The Role of the Minister's Wife,* divided literature about the minister's wife "into five categories: (1) self-help works, (2) autobiography, (3) biography, (4) fiction, and (5) general works."[2]

Commenting on these categories, he said:

> The first four of these present a rather consistent picture of her. However, for the most part it is a stereotyped picture. As such, it is one that is frequently superficial and possibly misleading as to what the wife of a pastor is really like. To be sure, these must meet the needs of many wives. These self-help books might well be described as "how to do it" literature.[3]

> One of the main points in which the nonfiction literature appears to be unrealistic is in its concept of the minister's wife as a person. It is with difficulty that one is able to see

her as an individual. She appears to be playing a character in which the script for the role has been written by tradition.[4]

Not only does Denton develop the idea that "the literature on the minister's wife is partly unrealistic,"[5] but he also develops the idea that it is idealistic. Referring to this characteristic, he says:

> The composite picture of her depicts a woman who is the very epitome of all that is gracious, tactful, lovely, righteous, pleasant, and friendly. She is a skilled financier who does wonders with her husband's limited salary, an understanding counselor to those seeking her help, a gracious hostess to those accepting the hospitality of her home, her husband's right arm when needed, and possessing the finesse of a diplomat in handling inter-personal problems both at home and in the church.
>
> Ideals are needed and possibly idealism is warranted at times, but an idealistic system must be recognized for what it is—an ideal—and cognizance must be taken of the fact that no one fulfills the ideal at all points. In fact, most wives would probably agree that the characteristics of the ideal minister's wife listed in some of the literature are much to be desired. Furthermore, it may be reasonable to expect a wife to fulfill the highest expectations in some areas, but unreasonable to expect this in all areas. With the apostle Paul, one is made to ask, "Who is sufficient for these things?" However, the attitude seems to be communicated to the reader that the *good* minister's wife possesses all these characteristics. Little attention is devoted to recognizing that few, if any, fulfill the ideal at all points.[6]

It's great to have ideals, but you need to be realistic. You won't be able to fulfill the idealistic concept of the minister's wife in every detail because you are human. One minister's wife said, "We need to remember that we aren't in competition with the angels."

When my husband and I were bringing up our sons in the

atmosphere and activities of a parsonage, we often said to them, "We want you to live this way not because you are children of a preacher but because you are Christians."

Similarly I say to ministers' wives, "You should aim to be all that God expects you to be as a Christian, a follower of Jesus Christ, and a child of God. God has high standards for His children, and He wants you to keep on learning and growing and maturing."

To foster this process of growth, you will need to study the Bible and learn to apply its principles to everyday living. Also, you will need to learn all you can about the ministry of the Holy Spirit in a believer's life and pray that His presence and power may be a reality in *your* life.

If you yield yourself to the indwelling Holy Spirit to be controlled by Him, you can relax as far as your role as a minister's wife is concerned, because He will create in you a joyous spontaneity of life which is unobtainable by your own efforts. You can relax and live naturally. I use the term *naturally* in the sense of "normally" because of the teaching presented in the New Testament about what is normal in the Christian life. John 7:38-39 illustrates what I mean. There it is recorded that Jesus said, "He who believes in Me, as the Scripture said, From his innermost being shall flow rivers of living water" (NASB). The refreshing flow of blessing from a Christian should be as constant and effortless as the flow of water from an artesian well.

Even so, you will need to be realistic about your role and recognize that you will never get to the place where you will be the "perfect" minister's wife, having reached the "ideal" which you, in the dreams of your youth, envisioned. But, as the years pass, you will be able to see that you have been developing as a Christian person and making progress on the road to spiritual maturity.

As you walk along this road, God will bless others through you without your having to "try" to be a blessing.

3

Feelings of Inadequacy

How friendly can a pastor and his wife be with the members of their congregation? Should a pastor and his wife have close friends, or are they to make up their minds that this can never be?

Questions such as these represent only one area about which young women who are wives of pastors feel uncertain.

Uncertainty and feelings of inadequacy, tensions and frustrations among pastors' wives without doubt contribute to the high rate of breakdowns referred to in a *Time* magazine article which appeared in 1961. While no one can give a definite percentage figure for such breakdowns, one minister's wife, whose letter I quoted in chapter 1, said, "At least 25 percent of us must be on the verge of nervous breakdowns."

I have already referred to tensions caused by a conflict between what is expected of the minister's wife by the congregation, her husband, and herself—*and* what *she* wants to be and do. She may also be torn between her concept of the "ideal" minister's wife and what she really is.

It is not uncommon for a minister's wife to be overwhelmed with feelings of inferiority. Among the reasons may be these:

1. She comes from a home which did not provide her with a Christian background.

2. She lacks a background of culture which would give her the assurance she is doing the right thing as far as etiquette is concerned, or which would give her poise in entertaining.

3. She doesn't have a college education.

4. She doesn't have biblical knowledge, and feels this lack when asked to teach a Bible class. One woman who wrote to me said, "I feel so unqualified. I have as many excuses as Moses had, as many excuses as anyone can think of."

5. She is without natural gifts of leadership.

Such inadequacies are not insurmountable. You can read books about the Christian home and etiquette and entertaining, plus no end of magazine articles which are constantly appearing on the subject. If you don't have a college education and want one, you can take some courses if a college is nearby which allows individuals to take less than a full academic load.

However, I would point out that there are men in the ministry who don't want a "brain" for a wife; they want a woman with a warm, outgoing, unselfish personality. She is a real asset. You can be a well-informed woman even if you don't have a college degree. You can be alive and alert mentally and know what is going on in the world and what the needs of our society are through reading current publications.

You can enrich your own inner man and be prepared for intelligent conversation and for Bible teaching by reading books of various kinds, and particularly by working through books designed to aid students of the Bible. You are more fortunate than most women, for you have a library in your home or in your husband's study from which you can make such selections.

Now, let's consider the question, "How friendly can a pastor and his wife be with the members of their congregation?"

First, I would point out that there is a difference between being friendly and intimate. You might want a definition of the word *intimate*. I found this one: "a relationship to a person which involves entertaining and being entertained in a social way with frequency."

Next, there is a difference between actively promoting an

intimate friendship and loving acceptance of friendliness. Don't feel that you need to turn down dinner invitations from your parishioners. On the other hand, acceptance of such invitations does not require a return invitation to the parsonage.

I heard of a pastor and his wife who were criticized by members of their congregation because after the church had spent a great deal of money remodeling and updating the parsonage, no one had seen the results of the expenditures. This pastor and his wife had never invited anyone of the congregation to the parsonage.

It's only fair to take into consideration the possibility that the attitude of this couple may have arisen out of their desire not to show favoritism. But they could have satisfied the wishes of the members of the congregation to see the parsonage after its face-lifting by arranging for an open house. At one church where my first husband was pastor the remodeling of the parsonage required three months and the expenditure of several thousands of dollars. After the remodeling was completed, we invited our people to a Sunday afternoon open house. They were delighted with what they saw, and I was gratified with their reactions because I had planned the color scheme and had made the living room and dining room draperies.

While it is understandable that a ministerial couple who jealously guard the privacy of their home might do so because they are reacting against the attitude some congregations have that the parsonage belongs to them, I think it is a mistake when a minister and his wife don't ever invite members of their congregation to their home.

Some members can visit as members of committees or boards which are invited to meet at the parsonage. However, there is a way of making it possible for all to visit in the home of the minister at some time or other. In a small church you could have an open house—perhaps on a special day like New Year's Day. In a larger church you could invite groups to the parsonage for Sunday evening after-church fellowship and serve light, simple refreshments. You could divide your congregation into groups. On one Sunday invite families whose last names begin with the letters *A* to *H*. On another Sunday invite families whose last names begin with the letters *I* to *O,* and so on. When your people see you and your husband in the setting of your home and in a different situation than at church, they will feel they know you a little better.

However, though it is ideal for a minister and his wife to open their home to their people on occasions such as I have mentioned, the members of the congregation ought to remember that even though the parsonage is owned by the church it is the minister's home while he is their pastor. Therefore, he should be accorded the same courtesies and privileges as any homeowner.

Let's return to the question of whether your husband and you should have "intimate" friendships with members of your congregation. If you do, what is involved? Jealousy, possibly. There is the possibility of suspicion that you will "use" your friends to attain your own ends. Then there's the possibility of a "disenchanted" friend who may become bitter and be a hindrance to the effectiveness of the pastor's influence.

Intimate friendships within your congregation may encourage situations which will be a bit delicate to handle when your husband moves on to another pastorate and these friends want him to return to officiate at weddings, funerals, and so on. While a warm feeling of affection for the former pastor is appreciated by him, the present pastor must be considered too.

I think it's best for a minister and his wife to cultivate intimate friendships with persons outside their congregation. Many ministerial couples enjoy such friendships with another such couple. The disadvantage of such an association is the tendency to engage in "shop talk." If you spend time developing friendships with persons in other professions you can widen your interests and gain new perspectives, which certainly is desirable for a minister—or anyone, for that matter.

To you who say you feel inadequate because you are not a natural leader, I would reply, "You don't have to be a leader." If all were leaders, who would be the followers?

Many women are gifted as helpers. I'm so glad the Lord included the gift of "helps" in the list of gifts of the Holy Spirit mentioned in 1 Corinthians 12:28.

Euodias and Syntyche, referred to by the apostle Paul in Philippians 4, have often been alluded to in sermons as two women who had a "falling out," who did not get along well together. But not much emphasis is placed on the fact that they were Paul's helpers in the sense of laboring with him in the spread of the gospel.

Paul recognized a woman named Phoebe when he wrote the epistle to the Romans (16:1-2), and spoke of her as "a succourer of many," as well as of himself. The word *succourer* is translated "helper" in some versions and "assistant" in others. This woman went to Rome on business, and the church there was asked to give assistance to her.

Dorcas was another first-century woman who helped in the church. She is described in Acts 9:36 as a woman "full of good works and of almsdeeds." The word *almsdeeds* refers to the kind things she did for the poor, including the sewing of garments for them (Ac 9:39).

Priscilla, wife of Aquila, was referred to by Paul in Romans 16:3 as one of his "helpers in Christ Jesus."

All Christian women, including wives of ministers, may be included among those who are helpers of those who preach the gospel. One way of helping which does not require the capacity to lead others is that of prayer (see 2 Co 1:11; Phil 1:19).

As you think of your inadequacies, meditate on the implications of this prayer:

> Lord, help me to change what can be changed,
> And accept what cannot be changed.
> And give me the wisdom to know the difference.

Many of our inadequacies can be remedied by study and spiritual and emotional growth.

4

Conflicts Related to Time, Energy and Children

"How do I find time to do all the things people of the church expect of me?" was one of a number of questions presented to me in a letter received from a pastor's wife several years ago. She said,

> Dear Mrs. Nordland: I am a minister's wife and the mother of five children, ranging in age from 3 to 15. I feel each one needs his mother, even the fifteen-year-old. I am expected by the church to carry on a complete schedule of church work, each and every day, and three to four nights a week. I feel that my children are the responsibility that God expects me to take care of first, but the church uses the Scripture, "Forsake all and follow Me." I cannot believe that our Lord meant it this way.
>
> In the past few days I have been especially frustrated by long telephone calls and have begun to keep track of the time spent on the telephone counseling with people. I would say it amounts to an average of 3 to 4 hours each day. I love people, and I love to help them when I can, but many times they call just to complain about another church member. True, this is not physical labor, but it wears me down emotionally, until I am so very tired. Then, of course, I have to work into the night to catch up on my housework, for if someone should come in and see dirty dishes in the sink the word is spread over the entire church, and I am severely criticized.

26

I think that I should add, to clarify some of these points I have made, that it is not my husband's fault. He pastors a church that will not support us. May I emphasize that they will not do this, for it isn't true that they cannot support us. So my husband has to work at a full-time job in addition to his responsibilities as a pastor. Incidentally, he gives the church as many hours as he does his job, which means a weekly total of 80 hours work for him. We have lived with these conditions for three years. Mrs. Nordland, does God really expect this of His ministers? My husband has a very good education. Shouldn't the laborer be worthy of his hire? Would we be shirking our responsibilty to God if, when we move to our next pastorate, we expect Him to provide us with a church that will support us?

I have covered more subjects than I intended when I began this letter. I should add, I suppose, that I am under a doctor's care for excessively high blood pressure caused by overwork and emotional tension.

What this woman revealed in her letter illustrates very well the conflict felt by a woman who is a pastor's wife. She is torn between what the church expects of her and what *she* feels she should be and do.

Any mother with five children ranging from three to fifteen year of age is carrying a heavy responsibility that requires of her more than she can accomplish in an eight-hour day. And then when she adds to her duties as homemaker the carrying of church responsibilities that require her to be away from home three or four nights a week in addition to the hours spent in daytime meetings for women, calling on parishioners with her husband, answering the telephone—and not only answering it but engaging in long telephone-counseling sessions with disturbed persons—she is carrying an exceptionally heavy load.

When I was in my twenties and early thirties I was very much involved in the work of the churches which my husband pastored. I had no conflict about such involvement because this was what I wanted to do. But as I look back, I see that I hired baby-sitters to care for my children more often than I now think I should have. For this reason I advise young wives of pastors to be sure to give plenty of time to their children. I tell them, "Your children will go through the most impressionable years of their lives—the preschool years—only once; they will go through the growing-up process only once. Give them the emotional security that children gain when Mother is there and available to them, when Mother is able to give more of herself because she hasn't taken on too many outside activities and hence is less hurried and harried, less tired."

But, since your husband's relationships with his congregation are important, you wouldn't want people to say, when he makes appeals for volunteers in various areas of the church work, "Why should I volunteer? His wife doesn't do anything in the church." From this viewpoint, it seems to me that you would want to engage in such service as you can without neglecting your children and without becoming exhausted.

Mr. Nordland tells me that in the churches he pastored, he would, on his first Sunday in the pulpit, explain that the church had hired him—not his wife. He made clear that they were not to expect more of her than would be expected of other women in the church, and that she would not be an officer of any of the organizations of the church but that she would cooperate and assist in any way she could. He also told his congregations that his daughters were normal children, and that more should not be expected of them than of the children of other church families.

William Douglas, who has written a book titled *Ministers' Wives,*[1] says that "clarification and testing of expectations is necessary on *both* sides of the congregation-minister's wife relationship. Minister-husbands must be involved, too, in terms of their expectations of the congregation, and of their wives and families. Wives need to understand their involvement in the ministry. Basic to all these considerations is an understanding of the covenant relationship of mutual care and concern.

"This is something quite different from a congregation making demands on a minister's wife and seeking to exploit her as a worker, with little concern for her as a person, woman, wife, and mother. It is quite different, too, from a minister's wife seeking to maintain her rights but minimize her responsibilities. Such a wife expects that others will provide the best for her in housing, finances, and courtesies but that they have no right to expect anything of her in return.

"When commitment, competence, and dialogical communication operate on both sides, then a congregation may grow in its capacity to care for others without dominance, and a minister and his family can grow in their capacity to be cared for without dependence."[2]

Mr. Douglas also says, "At the point of the call or appointment of a minister to a new pastorate, in particular, it would be useful if some means were provided to assist a congregation in clarifying its expectations of a minister and his family. . . . For example, for ministerial families with young children there should be realistic facing of the cost of baby-sitting for meetings attended by a minister's wife. Either expectations should be lowered or some provision of volunteer help and/or financial assistance made. The question should be raised as to whether it is considered necessary, or even desirable, for her to attend all of the women's groups of the church, and what sort of involvement in community life beyond the church may be desirable."[3]

When my correspondent said that the church used the scripture verse, "Forsake all and follow Me," as a basis for expecting her to carry as heavy a schedule of church responsibilities as she does, I referred to a Bible concordance so that I could locate the reference and read it in its context. I found that the words were not a direct command of the Lord but described what some of the disciples who were fisherman did when Jesus called them (Mt 19:27; Mk 1:18; Lk 5:11). When they forsook all, they left their boats and nets. In other words, they left their secular occupation. The application of these words to a mother's forsaking her first responsibilities (the care of her husband and children) certainly is not valid. Instead of applying these words to the minister's wife, the congregation might rather consider the desirability of making it possible for their pastor to leave his secular work by providing him with an adequate salary. When I replied to this woman's letter I said to her, "Presenting to God your desire that your next pastoral move will locate your husband in a church that will support him and his family fully is a proper prayer request."

I also included this advice:

"Since you say that you are under a doctor's care for excessively high blood pressure caused by overwork and emotional tension, you will need to be very realistic about how heavy a load you should carry.

"Don't be afraid to cut down on the length of the telephone conversations. I realize that you may be involved in more counseling than you might otherwise be called on to give since your husband is away during the day because of his secular work. If, as you indicate, many of the calls are from immature Christians who call to complain about another church member, you might be able to cut the conversation short by asking your caller, 'Have you talked directly to Mrs. So-and-so about this?' And if she hasn't, tactfully let her know that until she does talk to this other person you feel you should make no comment.

"If you consistently respond in this way to complaints about fellow church members, you will find yourself receiving fewer calls of this nature.

"When a caller goes on and on, you may have to cut her short with 'I'm sorry, but I just can't talk any longer.' And then

mention something which you must get done without delay.
And, from what you have written, I take it that there are always tasks calling for your attention."

Perhaps you will be helped in deciding how to handle the
problem of phone calls by a story I read in one of Anna
Mow's books, *Your Child*.[4] The story is about a minister's
wife who had been a professional woman in the field of religious education before her marriage. It was natural, therefore, that she was drawn into church activities more than
"housework," although she was conscientious in the affairs of
her household. Just before she went to the conference where
she met Anna Mow, she had overheard one of the parishioners
saying something about "the preacher's brats." She was
stunned. Could they mean her children? They did! This
opened her eyes to problems on her own doorstep to which
she had previously been blind. She now saw that her children
had deep rebellion against the church, and she faced the
fact that the most frustrating hours of the day were just before the children left for school in the morning and after their
return in the afternoon. She realized now that the morning
hour was the favorite telephone hour for the women of the
church because they were sure she was still at home then. No
wonder the children felt that the church was in competition
with them for the attention of their parents. They felt neglected and unloved. No wonder they rebelled against this in-
trusion!

After this mother saw where she had failed her children
she took drastic steps to correct the situation. She frankly
told her Sunday school class of women that she had overheard
the "brat" story. Then she thanked them for awakening her
to her responsibilities and asked them to help her turn the
minister's "brats" into the minister's children. The new rule
was that no one was to call her in the morning before the
children left for school, except in case of fire or death! The
same rule held for the afternoon hour when the children re-

turned from school. These hours were to be "children's hours" without any competition.

If you inform members of your congregation that there are specific periods of the day when you don't want to be called, they may pause to give second and third thoughts to the question of whether their particular phone call is really necessary. Rules about times when you prefer not to accept phone calls do not represent a selfish attitude. The solution of this problem has a bearing on your well-being and on your family life, and these two factors in turn have an indirect effect on the church.

5

Housekeeping

The picture of the "ideal" minister's wife conveys the idea that she manages her home well and keeps an immaculate house—accomplishments she achieves in spite of devoting many hours a week to church work.

Is this picture realistic? No!

What is the effect upon the woman who finds she cannot live up to it? She may have guilt feelings about her "failure" to conform to the ideal. She may worry about what people will think if they drop in at the parsonage and see dirty dishes in the sink or dust on table tops. She may fear that word will be spread over the entire congregation about her poor housekeeping.

In response to a plea for advice from the woman I have mentioned who had feelings like this, I told her that a woman with five children from ages three to fifteen to care for, would not find it possible to keep her house in "apple pie" order at all times. Especially was this true in light of the heavy load of responsibilities she was carrying as the wife of a pastor who worked at a secular job requiring forty hours a week. I said to her, "If people can't recognize that, they are very unrealistic." And I suggested that she shrug her shoulders, laugh, and say, "Well, I just can't please everybody! And besides, all that has been hurt is my pride!"

I also suggested that she lighten her work load by assigning household chores to her children in addition to making a schedule for herself.

As well as making a schedule, a woman must discipline herself to hold to it. However, she needs to be flexible enough to allow for interruptions. These can't be scheduled; they just occur.

I wasn't what is called "a perfect housekeeper" in the years when my boys were small and I lived in an eight-room house (large rooms at that!). This house had fifty-two windows which needed to be kept clean—and, of course, the curtains for those fifty-two windows. During that period of time I used to say I sandwiched my housework in between the meetings of the church. As far as the house was concerned, I did what showed the most.

When I knew that a missionary family of four was scheduled to stay at our home for two weeks, I really went on a housecleaning binge. And I felt rewarded for my efforts when the missionary wife commented, "Your house just sparkles."

During those years our church was unable to go ahead with projected building plans because of regulations of the War Production Board, so a building was rented for Sunday meetings and the Wednesday night prayer meeting. And the monthly women's missionary meeting was scheduled for the parsonage because we had a large living room—14 by 20 feet. Large parties were also held at our home. Among these were missionary showers at which the women gave to our missionaries household utensils, clothing, bedding, and various other items to outfit them for a five-year stay overseas. Such affairs would bring to our home as many as eighty-five women. One time, as I was getting ready for such a party, I washed four pairs of dining room curtains made of a rayon marquisette. Well, the curtains went to pieces in the water, practically dissolving. I had no choice but to rush downtown to purchase new curtains. As I remember, I didn't have the money to purchase new ones, for such an expense hadn't been included in our budget at that time. Fortunately, I was able to charge them to our account. Otherwise, I would have had to do without!

Of course, I could have done that, but somehow I just couldn't see having a party at our home with curtainless dining room windows.

Even though I wasn't a perfect housekeeper, I did have a daily flexible schedule designed to keep our home *looking* orderly, even though all the windows weren't freshly washed, the floors waxed, and the carpets vacuumed.

Here is the schedule:

1. Before you go to bed at night, survey the living room and family room and take glasses and cups to the kitchen.

2. In the morning, as soon as possible after breakfast, see to it that the table is cleared, the dishes washed and put away, and the kitchen put in order.

3. Make the beds. (As soon as your children are old enough, require them to make their own beds, put away their nightclothes, and give their room a weekly cleaning.)

If you follow such a plan, your house won't look too bad, even if you don't get to dusting the furniture. When I was a bride, my good Holland-Dutch mother-in-law, who was an immaculate housekeeper, gave me this advice: "If you keep things picked up and in their place, your house will look neat." And she lived up to that advice. In fact, you could never find yesterday's newspaper in her house. It was already disposed of.

If someone should call at your home and the children's toys are lying around or you haven't put away the freshly laundered and ironed clothes, you needn't feel embarrassed. Instead, let your attitude be this: "After all, work goes on in this house as well as in other homes—and play! Our home is not a showcase. It's a place where very human, down-to-earth persons live, love, work, play, and learn."

In a Christian home, of course, we can relate all of such activities to God, and seek to please Him in every area of our homelife.

THE CHRISTIAN HOME

How God must love a friendly home
Which has a warming smile
To welcome everyone who comes
To bide a little while!

How God must love a happy home
Where song and laughter show
Hearts full of joyous certainty
That life means ways to grow!

How God must love a loyal home
Serenely sound and sure!
When troubles come to those within
They still can feel secure.

How God must love a Christian home
Where faith and love attest
That every moment, every hour,
He is the honored Guest!

GAIL BROOKS BURKET

The atmosphere of your home is more important than the perfection of its furnishings, appointments, cleanliness and order. You can do only what can be accomplished within the dimension of time you have each day. God doesn't expect the impossible, and it isn't right for you to bring about a nervous breakdown by attempting to do more than can be accomplished within the limits of your time and strength.

When you find yourself becoming anxious about what people may say about your housekeeping, you might repeat to yourself this message from the Lord that was drummed into Amy Carmichael's consciousness by the rhythmic clickety-clack of train wheels on the tracks on a day when she was disturbed about a silly bit of gossip: "Let it be, think of Me. Let it be, think of Me."

Thoughts about our lovely Lord can bring peace in the

midst of inner turmoil. I have experienced this time and again, and that is why I recommend this kind of mental and spiritual exercise.

6

Reject Self-Pity

Since I have referred to the conflicts a minister's wife feels between what is expected of her and what she wants to be and do, to the tensions caused by her feelings of inferiority or inadequacy (for various reasons), and some of her problems, you may be wondering, "Aren't there any privileges? Aren't there any joys? Aren't there any ministers' wives who are without conflicts, who face their situation courageously, and who meet their problems as challenges and look upon them as situations where they can learn and grow?"

Yes, there are privileges; there are joys. There are women who love their role as a pastor's wife. One minister's wife expressed how she felt in this poem:

I'm glad that I'm a pastor's wife,
I truly count it joy
To daily walk and work with one
Who is in God's employ.

True, I sometimes feel resentment
That my time is seldom mine,
When I begrudge the time to pray,
"Lord, I would be *fully* thine."

Though I know the deep frustration
Of my housework never done,
Of seldom having time to read
Or do things "just for fun."

I do not know the boredom
Of empty, aimless days,
So though I'm often weary,
My heart is filled with praise.

Should we not count it joy to bear
The burden of another?
Then I blush with shame and whisper,
With needy youth or mother?

Is there not sweet satisfaction
In watching children grow
Into Christian youth and then go out
The gospel seed to sow?

So though my time is seldom mine,
The phone and doorbell ring,
I'm glad that I'm a pastor's wife,
It makes me want to sing.[1]

MARIAN VAN DAM

Later I discuss the joys, privileges and rewards of the woman who is a pastor's wife. However, I want to continue to discuss her problems—not to make it seem that her problems are worse than the problems of other women (many of them are the same), but to give answers to the problems.

One of them is the tendency to feel sorry for yourself because of the demands placed upon you just because you are a pastor's wife. I remember an occasion when I was engaged in conversation with an unmarried woman who had been in the business world for many years. I was sort of complaining about something connected with my role of pastor's wife. She commented, "It's well to remember that wives of business executives face in their roles some of the same demands that ministers' wives face."

I have since learned, from my reading on the subject, that a corporation may look over the wife of the prospective executive much as a church looks over the wife of the minister, considering whether she will be an asset or a liability to his ministry. Certain demands are made on each for entertaining, for attending social functions with her husband, and so on. For example, your position may require you to buy more clothes or more expensive clothes than you would buy if your position in life were less public.

Wallace Denton, in his book *The Role of the Minister's Wife,* referred to a study on the corporation executive's wife done by William Whyte in 1951 which indicated that some corporations consider their executives' wives almost as important as the executives themselves.[2]

One quotation from Dr. Whyte's study is thought provoking: "Management . . . has a challenge and an obligation to deliberately plan and create a favorable constructive attitude on the part of the wife that will liberate her husband's total energies for the job."[3]

Let's transfer that concept to the minister's wife. Is it not true that a favorable, constructive attitude on her part will liberate her husband's total energies for his job—a job that is vastly more important than that of a corporation executive?

Some corporations plan "wife programs" designed to extend the influence of corporations into the home. One well-known corporation conducted a series of wives' clinics to aid the wife in understanding and helping her husband. In like manner, a minister's wife can be helped in understanding her husband's role and her own by attending retreats for ministers' wives and special sessions for pastors' wives at conferences or denominational meetings.

The ideal corporation wife is characterized as highly adaptable, highly gregarious, and keenly aware that her husband belongs to the corporation. She is expected to have well-disciplined children, provide a relaxed atmosphere for the home, be a gracious hostess, avoid controversial attitudes, and have an agreeable disposition. She may be cautioned about appearing too intellectual or outstripping in other ways those with whom she associates. Of course, in the fishbowl existence in which the corporation wife is regarded as highly important to her husband's success, she is expected to dress attractively but conservatively.

Now that you know what is expected of a corporation executive's wife, perhaps you have come to the conclusion that what is expected of a pastor's wife doesn't seem too unreasonable. But you may not want to conform to an unrealistic, idealistic pattern because you fear that doing so will make you feel you have come out of the same mold as every other wife of a minister. However, you don't need to hide your personality behind a facade designed to please everyone. No, *you* are *you!* And God will use your personality in a way that He will use no other. But you can strive for excellence as you participate in the various activities of your life in the parsonage, in your church relationships, and in community contacts. Thus you will be a real help to the work of the Lord as carried on by your church under the leadership of your husband, a servant of God.

Sometimes the question is raised whether a woman who is going to fill the role of pastor's wife should have a divine call, just as her husband has had a divine call. An editorial in *Moody Monthly* in January, 1961, referred to a statement made by a state denominational paper which said that "most ministers' wives have never heard a divine call, they have simply married men who have." The writer of the editorial commented, "Such a conclusion fails to explain the very heart of the dedication we find in the wives of Bible-believing pastors wherever we go. And we suspect the secret of their striking service goes far deeper than personality or even devotion to their husbands."[4]

No opportunity to consider a divine call is given to women who are already married when their husbands decide to go into the ministry. When the question came up for the husband's prayerful decision, the wife's attitude may have been

that described by the words, "Whither thou goest, I will go."
A similar attitude is adopted by many single women as they
consider marriage to a man who plans to serve the Lord as a
minister of the gospel. They feel the husband's call to the
ministry includes his wife.

In my opinion, if a woman has a deep conviction that she
is in God's place for her, then she can look to God for
strength and wisdom and the grace to be the kind of person
God wants her to be. As she seeks wisdom from God, she will
know what priorities to set, when to say a firm no. Most
people who know pastors' wives would agree that most of
them are amazing persons—amazing for their stamina, their
versatility, their ability to live and work with others. It's true,
as one publication put it, that "the stresses and strains are
enough to stagger an Amazon," and that they lead an inexor-
able fishbowl existence in which they are expected to be
models to other women as a wife, mother, homemaker, hostess, churchwoman, and so on.

Even though the stresses and strains are great, once a woman
has established priorities on the basis of making distinctions
between what is desirable (what she would *like* to do) and
what is important (what she *ought* to do), she can then appropriate this promise: "I can do all things through Him
[Christ] who strengthens me" (Phil 4:13, NASB). That
means, in my opinion, "I can do all things [within God's will
for me to do] through Christ who strengthens me."

This verse is rendered in the Amplified Bible like this: "I
am ready for anything and equal to anything through Him
Who infuses inner strength into me, [that is, I am self-sufficient in Christ's sufficiency]."

And I like to associate 2 Corinthians 9:8 with that verse:
"God is able to make all grace abound toward you; that ye,
always, having all sufficiency, . . . may abound to every good
work."

7

Rejoice in Your Privileges

On occasion, when I have addressed women and girls at mother-daughter banquets, I have mentioned that, while home-making isn't glamorous, it does have its compensations and re-wards. This also holds true for the role of the minister's wife.

The uninitiated often view the role of a minister's wife as glamorous. This was true of a girl, a student at the Moody Bible Institute, whom I met for the first time during the insti-tute's annual Founder's Week conference. My husband and I had traveled to the conference with her parents, newcomers to our town who had begun attending our church. Their daughter's first words after being introduced to me, were these: "Oh, there's nothing I want to be more than to be a minister's wife!"

I was intrigued by her frankness and wondered why she thought being a minister's wife would be so wonderful. Was it because she viewed a minister as a charming, well-dressed person whose pulpit ministry would influence many lives? Was it because of the status she would have as the wife of a minister?

I think she was idealizing the position of a minister's wife. Of course, a minister's wife does enjoy many privileges, but she faces problems as well. As I have discussed some of these problems, you may have thought that I have been painting the picture of her role in dark colors. However, the life of a pastor's wife isn't all problems. Neither is it all privileges and

43

benefits. Her life is like any other person's life in that she has some dark days and some bright days, stormy days and days filled with sunshine. Life in some ways is like the weather, the sunshiny days far outnumber the stormy days.

A pastor's wife has the same problems with children and housekeeping and getting tired and discouraged that any other woman has. Added to these is the problem of her feeling that she must put the work of the church first. However, she needs to keep in mind that every woman fills more than one role, and she must learn to balance her roles.

The wonderful thing about being a pastor's wife is this: You are married to a man who is God's servant and you know he married you not only because he loved you but also because he thought you were a suitable companion for him in the work of the ministry. You can share his work in ways that other women do not share the work of their husbands. (Most men work away from home in an office, in a factory, out on the road as a salesman, and so on.) The minister's work is with people; and if his wife loves people, she has a ready-made opportunity to enter into the joys and sorrows of the people in their congregation along with her husband.

One of the greatest joys, in my opinion, is seeing a response to the Word of God in the lives of the people to whom you and your husband minister, both in decisions to accept Jesus as Saviour and in spiritual growth. Other joys in which I shared as a pastor's wife were these: rejoicing with parents when a new baby came into their home, and sharing in the happiness of a couple in whose wedding my husband participated.

Some of the sorrows which you share with your people are those which come as a result of spiritual lukewarmness or outright rebellion against God, illnesses which are incurable, broken marriages, bereavements. As I think back, I remember the time I accompanied my husband to a home to inform the wife that her husband had been killed that morning when the

earth-moving machine he was driving flipped over, pinning
him beneath it. I recall another time when we had to inform
three young persons in a family that their father, mother, and
younger sister had been killed in a car-train accident. Such
responsibilities are difficult, but they give the minister and
his wife an opportunity for spiritual ministries.

A pastor's wife can view a change of pastorate as a privilege
or a problem. Frequent moves used to be spoken of as a rather
peculiar characteristic of preachers' families, but since World
War II American society has become a mobile society. Ameri-
cans are on the move. First it was servicemen and their wives
and children. When the men returned from military service,
they took advantage of the GI bill of rights to obtain further
education and moved with their families to the college or university of their choice. Large corporations have increasingly
followed the practice of transferring junior executives from
place to place every few years. Recently I talked to a woman
who said she and her husband had been married thirteen
years, and during this period they had lived in ten different
locations. So, we pastors' wives need not feel that we are a
"special" group who are disadvantaged by frequent moving.

In fact, there are some advantages. One is that with each
move you will make new friends. Of course, it takes a little
while for new friends to become as dear as old friends. Another advantage for your husband may be that as he moves to
a larger church, he receives a higher salary and more assistance. Often in a larger church the minister's staff will include an assistant or associate pastor, a Christian education
director, a church secretary, and a minister of music. I think
the pastors of small churches—or of multiple charges—work
harder than the pastors of large churches. Of course, the
larger the church the larger the number of sick people there
are for the pastor to visit, and the more weddings and funerals. Also there will be a multiplication of meetings he must

attend or in which he must participate, but he has the assistance of a staff and a larger number of capable lay leaders.

When my first husband and I left his first pastorate to go to another church, it was an emotional experience so difficult that I said I didn't want to go through a similar experience again. On the day he announced his decision, his face was almost as white as a sheet when he came into the church auditorium prior to the morning service. He had been pulled this way and that in considering what decision to make. Now the time had come for him to read his letter of resignation. When he finished, in order to give himself time to control his emotions, he announced that the deacons would receive the morning offering. The deacons went the length of the aisles with tears coursing down their cheeks. And I sat at the back of the auditorium, sobbing. No wonder I said I didn't want to go through such an experience again! But we served at the second church twice as long as we had served at the first church.

While we were in our first pastorate our first three children were born. The people of the church were so kind as each new baby arrived, with gifts for the baby, including a high chair and a stroller. And many girls and young women offered their services as baby-sitters.

What compensations are there for a minister's wife other than to which I have referred?

I have mentioned in passing that she acquires new friends as she and her husband move from one church to another. In their new location she never has to wait to become acquainted, for people are anxious to meet her.

She enjoys prestige because of her husband's position. In one community where we were located, the ministers' wives were given honorary membership in the women's club. I didn't have time to attend many of their meetings, but I appreciated the club's thoughtfulness.

A pastor's wife is often invited out to dinner with her husband, and to practically all of the weddings as well as to many of the baby and bridal showers. These occasions give her opportunities for closer relationships with members of the congregation through sharing important events in their lives.

Special attention is given to the pastor's wife in various ways. I have received corsages on my birthday and a gift from the congregation on our wedding anniversary. In two of the churches my husband pastored we received generous cash gifts at Christmastime.

One of the greatest compensations for a minister's wife is her growth as a person as she relates to the people in her husband's congregation. It requires tact, forbearance, a great deal of love, and a sense of humor.

I would advise churchwomen: Don't expect too much of your pastor's wife in areas of service in the church which other women can fill, for instance, in the church kitchen and nursery. If your pastor's wife has a special aptitude for teaching the Bible, recognize that as her sphere of service. Recognize also that she has a ministry that no one else in the church can render: that of maintaining her home as a haven of rest for her busy, often overworked husband and accompanying him on some of his calls. She has a ministry of prayer with him and for him. She shares the hurts that come to him, and she encourages him.

So, when you pray for your minister, pray for his wife and children.

Perhaps you can think of some practical down-to-earth ways to help her and make her lot a little easier, a little happier.

> Happy are those who make others happy,
> including your pastor's wife.

8

The Parsonage

Perhaps you have read, as I have, books by authors who described life in a parsonage forty or fifty years ago. These give revealing pictures of life in a minister's family in another generation, and some of the incidents recounted are highly amusing.

In the past it was customary for most churches to furnish a home for the minister and his family which was called the parsonage, manse, or the rectory, depending upon the denomination of the church. In recent years, more and more churches have given to men whom they call to serve as their pastor the option of purchasing their own home.

While placing a minister and his family in a home owned by the church has certain advantages, there are definite disadvantages. One of the chief ones, as I have experienced, is this: If the man of the house should die before his wife, she isn't left with the asset of a home. When my first husband died, we had been married thirty years. Most couples who have been married that long have a large equity in a home or have paid off the mortgage on their home.

When churches provided a parsonage, this provision used to be reflected in the minister's salary. Under these circumstances a layman might say to a minister who compared his salary with someone else's, "But you don't have to pay rent or make payments on a house!" However, that part of the minister's salary represented by house rental was lost to the minister as far as planning for his future financial program was concerned. Today many churches include in the church budget a rent allowance which the minister can use to rent an apartment or house or to purchase a home. If he does the latter, he will be building up an equity for the future. True, he will have to pay his own repair bills, taxes, insurance, and utilities (if the church makes no allowance for these, as some do). So, even though the church provides a housing allow- ance, this item in the church budget is not entirely an extra expense. The church will no longer have the expense of the upkeep of the parsonage and insurance on it, nor will it have thousands of dollars tied up in a parsonage.

For the minister there are these advantages when a church provides a housing allowance: (1) He can decide on the size of the house he wishes to occupy, which in turn will af- fect expenses involved in heating and furnishing the house. (2) He and his wife can enjoy the good feeling of home own- ership. (3) They can decorate as they please and modernize as they wish (as their income allows).

One of the disadvantages of a minister's owning his home is the difficulty he may encounter in selling the house when he makes a change of pastorates. Sometimes it takes six months to a year to dispose of a house. Meanwhile, he will be faced with the necessity of buying one in his new area.

Here are ten questions which members of a congregation should ask themselves if their church provides a parsonage for their minister:

1. Does the parsonage need painting inside and out?
2. Do those stains on the walls and ceilings represent a roof leak?
3. Is the kitchen an obsolete "woman killer"? Are the stove and refrigerator more than fifteen years old?
4. Has the bathroom been modernized?
5. Is the furnace automatic? Does it keep the house warm enough in winter?

6. Is the wiring safe? Are there enough outlets to run the appliances used in most homes?

7. If the furniture is church-owned, is it comfortable and reasonably attractive?

8. Does the minister have a quiet place to meditate and prepare sermons?

9. How does the parsonage compare to other homes in the neighborhood?

10. Would you and your family like to live there?

These questions appeared in *This Week* magazine in an article titled "What Ministers Hate Most About the Ministry" and written by Jhan and June Robbins.[1] What was hated most? Not the long hours for meager pay but the "homes" provided for them. It was an eye-opening article about a special housing crisis.

A few weeks later *This Week* reported that the article brought a flood of comments from ministers and church members, most of whom echoed the sentiments of the clergymen quoted in the article. Others felt that the rewards of a minister's life outweighed the housing problem. Still others reported that their housing situations were satisfactory. The most interesting letter of all, in the opinion of the editors, was from the wife of a Baptist pastor. She wrote:

DEAR MR. EDITOR:

Take it from a girl who grew up in parsonages, who wrote on her fifth grade theme "When I grow up I am going to marry a minister" and who did just that, one of the things I love most about the ministry is the parsonage.

I have lived in parsonages in half a dozen states all across our nation. And I have visited dozens and dozens of many denominations. What is it that I like about parsonages?

Most of all I love the man of God whose life I share in our parsonage. I like to think that he chose me because he thought I was fit to share this good life with him, to make our home an example of what God can do through one family living in His house. I'm proud to mend his clothes, listen to his problems and make this house a haven from the storm of life. . . .

I love the funny, good assortment of folks who come to our door for weddings, asking for or bringing food, wanting encouragement or just plain fellowship. I love the good and the bad all put together like a great jig-saw puzzle of humanity. They all belong in our house because we share our house with God and his servant.

I love moving into a parsonage. No minister's family is ever a stranger in a new town. The minute you move in someone says "That's *our* minister" or "Those are *our* preacher's kids." We never have to elbow our way in, we just belong. I have yet to move into a house that women of the church had not scrubbed and stocked with food for moving day. The good men of the church have always been on hand to help the movers. I deeply appreciate this. I often say to my children, "See how lucky we are to be living in a parsonage."

And I love the house itself. Some folks live in one house all their lives. I love the adventure and the challenge of a new house with its odd assortment of windows and that extra room you hadn't planned would be there. The minute we're called to a new parish we all begin planning. I have yet to see a congregation unwilling to let us redecorate to suit our tastes. We have helped to build one new parsonage and every parsonage where we have lived has received some face-lifting during our stay.

Show me a parsonage which does not respond to a little imagination and love and ingenuity. We are good at papering and painting and love the smell of fresh paint. No congregation yet has failed to respond to an invitation to sample my Norwegian cookies, even if we do suggest they wear work clothes and bring along brushes!

Of all the parsonages I have visited, I have yet to see a really well-trained, capable pastor without a decent home. Our denomination is short over 5,000 ministers. Most other Protestant denominations have a similar shortage of trained ministers. And it is becoming almost impossible for a church with a poor parsonage to get a pastor. At present we have in our vicinity two churches—both with new parsonages—which have been without pastors for some time.

In order to be ordained in most Protestant denominations a minister must have four years of college and three years of seminary. Many have much more education. My husband and I share six degrees.

Any number of higher paying jobs are open to a minister. He does not stay in the ministry because of the pay, the parsonage or the position. He stays because of a divine call; because he finds fulfillment for the greatest of life's goals. He truly believes: "Seek ye first the kingdom of God, and his righteousness; and all these things shall be added unto you."

Parsonages, God bless 'em.[2]

And I would add, God will surely bless the persons who live in the parsonage when they have an attitude like that—when they thank God for their blessings and don't dwell as much on the disadvantages of being in the ministry as on the compensations that outweigh the disadvantages and on the privilege of serving God in this way.

9

How Rich Is the Child of a Minister!

For many years I enjoyed the writing of columnist Dorothy Thompson without knowing that she was the daughter of a minister. This fact about her came to my attention when I read an article written by her bearing the title "I'm the Child of a King."[1] Because it is so beautifully written and because I found it so inspirational, I share it with you.

> In recent months I have seen a number of articles in church and lay publications calling attention to the miserable salaries paid to Protestant ministers. One article (*This Week* Magazine, February 1, 1959) bore the challenging title, "Must the Parsonage Be a Poorhouse?" and asserted that the average ministerial salary reported in a recent nation-wide survey was $4436 per year, or $85.30 per week, and that many parishes pay as low as $70.00 weekly.
>
> The author found this "shocking" and asked whether this was enough to pay a man who may have spent seven university years preparing for his calling, and one who works 60 to 80 hours a week, and who "hears the unhappiest problems life has to offer." The author remarked that "there are other noble ways to serve mankind and raise a family in decency, too: medicine, teaching, social welfare. . . . We may be inviting the disaster of having none but the timid, the inept and the fanatic to preach in our pulpits . . . if we want good religious leadership, we must be willing to pay for it."
>
> I am not opposed to better salaries for ministers, but in

this article, and in others like it, several of the chief heresies
of our times are reiterated, and in the most malapropos connection. One such heresy is that standard of living and
standard of life are the same thing. Another is that there is
no essential difference between "medicine, teaching, social
welfare" and the ministry. There are, of course, profound
differences. The ministry is service to God and via that service to humanity, reached through the soul. The other services can be performed by atheists. Another heresy is that
service to the Lord and Master of one's life can be measured
in years of preparation, in man-hours—or, indeed, measured
at all.

Although it is referred to as a "calling," by every
inference the author thinks of the ministry as a *career,* in
which one rises according to the various influences one is
able to mobilize, and in which parishioners get what they
pay for—no more, no less.

I wonder whether those who write this way really think
of what they are saying. If there were to be a minimum salary
of, say, $15,000 a year for all college-educated ministers, is
it likely that this would be accompanied by a great wave of
religious enthusiasm and revival? I should guess that just the
opposite would happen: the pulpits would be crowded, not
with zealots for God but with young careerists calculating
the ministry to be a better bet than most other "professions."

The history of the church does not bear out the notion
that we would have better religious leadership were its exercise a richer sinecure. On the contrary, the church has re-
peatedly been purified and strengthened by persecution and
even martyrdom. A belief that no one will die for, let alone
sacrifice for, becomes a belief that no one will live for or
live by.

The religious life has always been one of *voluntary* poverty
and sacrifice. In the more admirable parishes with which I
am familiar, country and urban, the minister usually has a
material standard of living about equal to the average of his
parishioners, though his moral and intellectual standard is
often superior to that of any of them. Religious leadership

is not exercised by public-relations build-ups, by the number
of lodges and community organizations of which the pastor
is a member, by the functions he performs outside his church
in behalf of the community, by the members he proselytes
from other churches, or by the inches of space assigned him
in the local press.

Religious leadership is a quiet thing, and the best of it is
unrecorded. It is manifest in the homes that do *not* break up,
in the young people who do *not* go astray, in the material
and spiritual crises that are met without public knowledge,
in those persons who meet misfortune and even death
serenely.

A community with great religious leadership is one im-
bued with love, fragrant with Christian charity, calm in inner
communal security—and such leadership cannot be had by
advertising for it on the money market. It is rare in any case.
But since we need not be without some insight into the lives
of saints, we do know that it is never to be found in those
concerned to any appreciable degree with money.

Miss Thompson observed that she was able to speak of the
ministry with some knowledge and authority, even though her
memories were drawn from the rather remote past.

For the first fourteen years of my life—until I left home
to live for the most of each year with aunts and go to
school in Chicago—my home was one of a series of Methodist parsonages in Western New York small towns. During
that time my father's salary never exceeded $1000 per year
and the use of a furnished parsonage. Sometimes fuel was
also provided—coal for the hand-stocked hot-air furnace
that transferred little heat to the second floor, and sometimes for a supplementary sitting-room stove and the kitchen
range.

My father seldom received his full salary in cash and
never retained all of it. A "tithe" was set apart immediately
for the missions of his church and his own (sometimes
whimsical) charities. His parishes were usually wide, including many farm folk who were richer in food than in cash

and often made their contributions to the church in the form of culled hens, eggs, or part of a side of beef or veal. Parishioners short in cash but long in good will made other payments in kind.

Nowadays one of the problems, I hear, that vex ministers is "car expense." Many feel they should have car allowances, as salesmen do. That problem did not bother my father. He had no car—nor did many other people in the days of which I write. Yet he did much more home-visiting, covering a lot of ground, than is customary today. In fine weather these visits were performed by bicycle; he thought nothing of pedaling twenty or thirty miles in a day. In inclement weather he made his calls by horse and buggy or horse and sleigh or "cutter," invariably borrowed from a church member. This custom gave us a considerable stable of alternatively used steeds, most of them distinguished by a singular lack of spirit, which was, perhaps, just as well, for though my father could drive, he was not an accomplished horseman. At any rate, the use of "Prince" or "Cap" or "Molly" rated, and quite properly, as a contribution to the ministry without money changing hands.

When I, a little older, protested such offerings, my father's eyes wrinkled in the corners, and he reminded me that our Lord and Master had made His triumphant entry into Jerusalem on a borrowed ass.

After presenting some colorful pictures of life in the five parsonages in which she lived before she was fourteen, Dorothy Thompson observed:

> From a dollars-and-cents viewpoint one could have called ours a "poorhouse" existence. In terms of food, clothing and shelter we had little more than the inmates of any "poor farm," on an income that translated into terms of today's cost of living amounted to about $68 a week for a family of five. But we certainly had the "decencies" of life. Our bodies, our clothing and our homes were clean, and food was Spartan but adequate.
>
> But was that *all* we had?

Oh, no!

We had a freedom characteristic of royalty: freedom from talk about money. I never heard money discussed in my father's house or used as a standard of measurement of ourselves or others. When, as children, we asked for things the household could not afford, we were told so; and although the telling no doubt brought pangs, they were not bitter. For relative wealth or poverty was not linked with relative superiority or inferiority.

There is a kind of complete humility that, in a sense difficult to define, equals complete pride; especially if pride, as I think it does, equates with total indifference to the impression one makes on others. My father was trying to keep up with a standard much higher than that of the Joneses.

Father's "call" to the ministry had come from the mightiest force in the universe, from its Author Himself. In my childish mind father's Boss was God; and He was a Boss of Whom or to Whom father never complained—even though, as I sometimes later thought, he *might* have complained of the episcopal system that, in fact, determined his livelihood. But I did not think much of that either. For a modest poverty seemed implicit in the ministry. How could one live in even relative luxury and serve a Master Who, unlike the foxes of the earth or the birds of the air, had no place to lay His head? Materially, our family was as well off as most of my father's parishioners, and to be markedly better off would not have seemed to him fitting.

When one is working for God, for the solace, support and redemption of souls, one is not engaged in collective or individual bargaining, nor can one keep a time clock. I knew my father was better educated than most of his friends and neighbors, but that had nothing to do with his rating a higher income, for he also was *better* than they and better than we—by common consent. We children had the security of this knowledge and of our parents' solicitous love.

In that parsonage poorhouse we also had books. In the evenings after early supper my father read aloud, not to us but to himself and my mother. Her hands were never idle to hold a book. They darned our heavy ribbed cotton stockings over a polished wooden egg, or let down tucks in petticoats or drawers, and patched or darned household linen, or even did "useless" things as well, embroidering "fancywork" to adorn the dining-room table or a shabby chest of drawers, or making a dress for my favorite doll from one of mine that had just enough whole cloth left in it for that purpose. And while her fingers were busy, Father read aloud.

I would be playing, like as not, on the floor, cutting out paper dolls or cardboard furniture for a doll's house, or doing an acrostic or rebus from St. Nicholas magazine, paying little heed to the reading, until some phrase or cadence of words, or plot of story, would divert me to listen. . . .

Here, long before I encountered them in school, I heard Evangeline and Hiawatha, School-Days and Snow Bound. Here, lying on my stomach, head propped in hands, floor playthings forgotten, I first met Little Nell and Little Dorrit, David Copperfield and Oliver Twist, Rob Roy and Ivanhoe, first heard of Hamlet's tragic dilemma, . . .

Often, listening, I cried the griefless tears of childhood that spring to the eyes with the majesty and beauty of only half-comprehended words. What did I know of the blind Milton, gone over two hundred years before my birth, whose light was spent ere scarcely more than half his days, complaining that the talent it was death to hide lodged in him useless—the talent he would fain put at the service of his Master—and then ceasing his complaint with the never-to-be-forgotten words:

> God doth not need
> Either man's work or his own gifts; who best
> Bear his mild yoke, they serve him best;
> 　　his state
> Is Kingly. Thousands at his bidding speed
> And post o'er land and ocean without rest:
> They also serve who only stand and wait.

Oh, the brave blind poet! I would think, interrupting to ask more about him, learning more, and rejoicing then that the

wonderful poem had been written *after* he became blind.
And oh, the kingliness of God!

As He was in Milton's immortal verse, so was He in the
hymns that filled so much of our lives.

My father had a beautiful tenor voice and would always
liefer sing than preach. So, in addition to poetry and prose
in our "poorhouse" parsonage homes, we had song.

My mother had started to study piano after her marriage,
before she was twenty. She could at least pick out the main
chords of songs and that was enough to start father and the
rest of us off. . . .

The hymns I loved best as a small child were not the
greatest ones, but rather those written for children, the im-
mortals being often beyond my comprehension. Yet their
majestic words and music moved me then as now, as they
have moved people of every race and clime for scores or
hundreds of years. . . .

My father thought that the greatest hymn written in English was Isaac Watts' When I Survey the Wondrous Cross,
and for sheer adoration it is surely without peer. I can remember the strange, holy sense of wonder, mystery and
beauty it evoked in me as a child, and that I could not sing
it without bursting into inexplicable tears.

> See from His head, His hands, His feet,
> Sorrow and love flow mingled down!
> Did e'er such love and sorrow meet,
> Or thorns compose so rich a crown?

With such a hymn in one's ears one was unlikely to complain that supper was only bread and jam and "cambric"
tea.

Dorothy Thompson quoted another song which was perti-
nent to the theme of her article:

> My Father is rich in houses and lands,
> He holdeth the wealth of the world in His hands,
> Of rubies and diamonds, of silver and gold,
> His coffers are full; He has riches untold.

> I'm the child of a King,
> The child of a King,
> With Jesus my Saviour
> I'm the child of a King,

She recalled how they "sang it with faith, affirmation and enthusiasm," and closed her article with this question: "Which was I, really? 'As poor as a church mouse,' the child of a 'parsonage poorhouse,' or the child of a King?"

The answer, of course, is obvious. She was a child of the King.

If the confidence that you are a child of the King imbues your life, then you can rejoice in your spiritual resources and the many privileges you enjoy, and can go through life without self-pity, no matter how limited your material resources. And you won't need to feel sorry for your children as they grow up in a parsonage, for you can enrich their lives through the "climate" or "tone" you and your husband provide in your home.

10

Finances

It's not considered good etiquette to talk about money matters—to discuss a person's salary or what you paid for an article of clothing or a piece of furniture. In spite of this rule I'm going to plunge into a woman-to-woman conversation about the minister and his wife and their attitude toward financial matters.

Sometimes the very lack of money may cause one to be preoccupied with it. When a person is hungry, he thinks primarily about food (how true this is when you're on a reducing diet!). When a person is broke, he thinks about money. Likewise, ministers and their wives who are feeling the pressures of living on an income which they judge to be insufficient for their needs may become preoccupied with financial matters. So they find the subject of their needs slipping into their conversation with others even though they may have said to themselves in private, "Now, we're not going to mention our needs. This is something between us and God." Still, they can't help but *think* about their needs.

A minister's wife is apt to become resentful about her husband's "low salary," especially if she is convinced that the church *could* pay her husband a higher salary. It is hard for her to accept statements she hears some persons make which emphasize the compensations a minister and his family receive which are not material. She can even feel resentful when someone mentions the spiritual qualities that can be developed during times of financial stringency—humility, for instance.

61

A story that has been told again and again through past years is that of the deacon who prayed to the Lord saying, "Lord, you keep him humble, and we'll keep him poor."

Someone has said that low salaries do not breed humility; they breed humiliation. Any pastor who is a real man wants to provide well for his wife and children just as any other self-respecting man does.

True humility is better tested when a man has an adequate salary. To have the option of what you do with an adequate income or a more than sufficient income is a true test of your mettle. When you're poor you don't have the opportunity to make choices about the expenditure of money that the affluent have.

Regarding humility in a preacher as related to his income, I can't help but think of an incident which occurred during the first year I was a pastor's wife. I was completely happy living in the large, drafty, seventy-five-year-old house that was the parsonage. For the first few months that we were married we had no car. Then a friend of Cornelius Beerthuis, my first husband, gave him a 1926 Chevrolet touring car (the kind we had to put side curtains on for rainy and cold-weather driving). This car had been taken in as judgment on a debt by a businessman in Grand Rapids, Michigan, and he gave it to us. We were delighted with it. One day when my husband called at the home of a farmer who was attending our church services, his neighbor noticed the car in which "a visitor" drove into this farmer's driveway. The next day the neighbor asked, "Who visited you yesterday?" The farmer replied, "Oh, that was our pastor." The neighbor exclaimed, "My, he must be a humble man!"

We laughed when we were told about this conversation. My husband remarked, "I'm driving that car not out of *humility* but out of *necessity*."

When we had finished school and were beginning our service for the Lord we were so thankful to be engaged in the

Lord's work that we didn't think about financial arrangements with our employer (the church we served) as much as it seems young people entering upon their life's work now do. I suppose the reason for the change in attitude is not a change that could be ascribed to a lesser degree of dedication but to the changing climate of the world around us. Numerous social reforms have been effected in the last thirty or forty years—social security, old-age insurance, labor legislation involving collective bargaining, all of which makes everyone more conscious of what are called the fringe benefits of a job.

Nowadays when a church calls a pastor, the call spells out the economic arrangements: whether a parsonage is furnished, the salary, car allowance, housing allowance if a parsonage is not provided, payment of utilities, provision of a sum which can be invested for retirement purposes to add to the benefits of the social security program. Usually the call indicates how many weeks' vacation will be granted and how many weeks the pastor will be allowed to use for speaking engagements elsewhere, and so on.

In our first pastorate, my husband paid all pulpit supplies when he preached at other churches or took a vacation. The salary was $1,200 a year, and there were times when the congregation was unable to pay the entire amount agreed upon because our country was going through an economic depression. The depression is an era which young people of today can't understand, for they haven't experienced anything like that. It was a time when tens of thousands of people were unemployed, when savings in bank accounts were frozen, when some wealthy (formerly wealthy) men committed suicide because of their losses in the stock market. They couldn't face life without money.

I remember reading about a couple who, during that period, stood at their window, looking at the sunset, arms about each other's waist. The man turned to his wife and said, "Well, dear, we've lost practically everything, but we still have each other and God."

Yes, to have faith in God, to know Him and to be confident that we never walk alone because He has said, as we read in Hebrews 13, "I will never leave thee, nor forsake thee," is of inestimable value. With such faith we can say with great assurance, "The Lord is my helper, and I will not fear what man shall do unto me."

In the Greek language two negatives serve to strengthen a negation. The first phrase I quoted, "I will never leave thee," could be translated, according to Kenneth Wuest, teacher of New Testament Greek at the Moody Bible Institute for many years, "I will not, I will not cease to sustain and uphold thee."[1] But then when you consider that the next words, "nor forsake thee," come from a phrase in which three negatives precede the word for "forsake," which means "to abandon, leave helpless, leave destitute, leave in the lurch, let one down," you realize you have a tremendous promise, one of *triple* assurance. It is, "I will not, I will not, I will not let thee down, leave thee in the lurch, leave thee destitute, leave thee in straits and helpless, abandon thee."[2]

Really, what are financial stringencies compared to such trials as persecution, incurable illness, death of a loved one, renouncing of the Christian way by someone close to you? Money ought to be the least of our worries. Someone has said, "Money can bless or curse. . . . You can be blessed abundantly while carrying a very thin wallet."

My husband doesn't approve of "poor-mouthing." That's a term which describes the person who talks as if he is poor, hard up, barely able to manage financially, needing to do without this or that because he doesn't have enough money. All too frequently a person who is guilty of "poor-mouthing" hopes that it will result in special gifts to him.

When we "poor-mouth" we dishonor the one whom we serve. It's like telling people that the Lord is not taking care of us properly. I recognize that it is God's people who often fail in providing adequately for God's servants, and for this lack of love and concern they must some day give an account to God, the one who will judge Christians for sins of omission as well as sins of commission. If God's people fail to properly support God's minister, then he and his wife can learn lessons in faith by looking to God for the supply of their needs from another source. They can be sure that He will not "let them down" and will use other means to supply their needs.

I found this to be true during the years I was the wife of a pastor as well as during the five years I was a widow and my speaking engagements represented one way of earning money. Some women's organizations were very unrealistic in deciding the amount of the check or cash handed to me in a sealed envelope. Evidently they did not take into account the amount of time I spent in preparation for the message I gave, the amount of time spent in driving to their place of meeting, and the cost of driving. Some women have said to me, "Oh, but you are in the Lord's service!" But I had to pay rent and telephone, light, and gas bills; I had to pay for a car, keep it in repair and the tank filled with gas, and I had to dress appropriately for public appearances. None of these expenses was less because my means of earning a livelihood was considered a service for the Lord. Are not all Christians serving the Lord, including the women who arranged for me to come and their husbands, even though they were engaged in secular work? These women did not feel it was wrong for them or their husbands to be paid adequately.

I was so relieved on one occasion when I was unburdening my heart on this subject to a Baptist pastor's wife. She said, "When a church calls a man to be their pastor, business matters are discussed and an agreement is reached concerning economic matters." She added, "It doesn't make his ministry any less spiritual to have discussed such matters." Since then I have felt less reluctant to discuss financial matters when those who are making arrangements for me to speak to their group ask me about such matters.

One woman to whom I wrote about the driving expenses involved, after delaying the writing of such a letter because of my reluctance to mention finances, said when I sat next to her at the banquet, "We are so glad you wrote to us as you did, for we like to have speakers and other talent come to our church from Chicago. We just had never thought about the item of driving expense." Not only did I feel relieved to know my explanation was well received, but I was glad to know I had been used in a process of educating them, which in turn would result in better arrangements for other Christian workers.

Perhaps in some situations a pastor may feel impelled to speak to the governing board of his church about his family's financial needs, even though he is reluctant to do so, and educate them in their responsibility to support God's servants.

I take the liberty of referring once again to the pastor whose wife told me he was working forty hours a week at secular work in addition to forty hours a week in his pastoral work. She said this church *could* support him but didn't. She didn't state the size of the membership of their church. Sometimes the number of members has a bearing on how well the church can support their pastor. However, a church with a small membership could be composed of members who themselves enjoy a very comfortable standard of living and hence could, if they gave a tenth of their income to the local church, support their minister and his family better than they do.

Many years ago I was present at the installation of the new pastor of a church where the membership was not large. But in the small group of Christians was at least one member who was a millionaire, and several others were wealthy, judging by the positions they held and the standard of living they enjoyed. The late Dr. M. R. DeHaan, well-known radio Bible teacher, gave the charge to the local congregation at the installation service. I remember his telling them that they should not keep their preacher at the lowest economic level represented in the congregation, nor at the highest, but that they should support him at the median level of income of the congregation. I think his idea was a good one.

If a church will respond positively to the teaching of Scripture about their responsibility to adequately support their minister, I am sure the result will be spiritual growth for the church. Spiritual blessing and maturing are the normal outcome of facing up to our responsibility and assuming it. Self-denial may be required for church members to give as they ought to in order to meet their financial responsibility for the support of their pastor and his family. Furthermore, faith will need to be exercised when a congregation takes such a forward step in obedience to God. However, when we exercise faith and practice self-denial to obey God's direct commands or to practice the principles found in Scripture, we can be sure of God's blessings upon us as individuals and as a church. I am strongly persuaded that when a pastor in a situation like the one I have mentioned is relieved of the necessity for secular work, the work of the church will go ahead by leaps and bounds because the pastor will be freed to spend more time in Bible study, sermon preparation and prayer, all of which will result in a strong pulpit ministry. And when the pastor is able to spend more time in visitation, this in turn may result in a numerical growth in church attendance and membership.

We can infer from the record of the appointment of the first deacons (see Ac 6) that those who are responsible for spiritual leadership ought to be relieved of responsibility for secular—or material—concerns. The apostles informed the Christians that other activities had a prior claim on them. They said, after asking for the appointment of seven men of honest report, full of the Holy Ghost and wisdom, "But *we* will give ourselves continually to prayer, and to the ministry of the word." Kenneth Taylor paraphrases, "Then we can spend our time in prayer, preaching, and teaching."

The spiritual values which a dedicated pastor can contribute to a church when he can devote an adequate amount of time to prayer and to Bible study, both for feeding the springs of his own spiritual life and for preparation for preaching and teaching, will far outweigh anything a church might give to him in the way of financial remuneration. There is scriptural basis for this statement. The apostle Paul wrote to the Corinthian church, "If we have sown unto you *spiritual* things, is it a great thing if we shall reap your *carnal* things?" (1 Co 9:11).

Professor F. F. Bruce, in his expanded paraphrase of *The Letters of Paul,* has rendered this verse this way: "We sowed a good crop among you—a spiritual crop. Is it a great matter that we should reap a material harvest from you?"[3] Paul spoke in this chapter of his being cared for in material things as a right which he personally did not use. Nevertheless he maintained the principle here and in several other sections of the Scriptures, evidently for the sake of other servants of God, both in the first century and down to the present time.

In a report issued in 1967, on practical problems of ministers I found that demands on the minister's time head the list of his problems. Next was concern about youth work—with more than half of the ministers questioned saying that they felt they "should spend more time" working with youth. Third was this problem: "He's still trying to make ends meet." The comments were these: "The salary situation seems to be improving modestly. The median annual salary in 1962 was $5,029, excluding parsonage allowance. The current survey shows that yearly salaries have increased by $885, certainly a trend in the right direction. At the present time, 57 percent are saying that money for day-to-day living expenses 'just meets my needs.' It is no wonder that the average minister continues to be concerned about being able to afford sending his children to college. Of the ministers surveyed, 74 percent indicated that financing college for their children is a problem. One third of all ministers have children of high school age, with college expenses looming just ahead."[4]

The chart that accompanied this report showed that in 1967, 10 percent of ministers were earning under $3,000, almost 20 percent were in the $3,000 to $5,000 bracket, and almost 50 percent were in the bracket embracing $5,000 to $7,000. A little over 20 percent earned $7,000 to $10,000.

So you can see that ministers are not in the affluent class, despite the fact that most of them have four years of college education plus three years of seminary—and sometimes more education than that. No wonder it's a temptation for ministers' wives to become resentful because of their economic plight! No wonder many of them decide to go to work outside their homes.

But there's another way: to learn contentment. Again and again during times of financial stringency when I was a minister's wife I had recourse to two passages of Scripture. One was Hebrews 13:5, "Let your conversation [turn of mind] be without covetousness [or free from the love of money]; and be content with such things as ye have: for he [God] hath said, I will never leave thee, nor forsake thee." The other passage was Philippians 4:11-12: "I have learned, in whatsoever state I am, therewith to be content. . . every where and in all things I am instructed both to be full and to be hungry, both to abound and to suffer need."

And I would think I had learned the lesson of contentment, but time and again I had to learn that lesson once again. It wasn't always easy, but it was good discipline for me to face the challenge of being content while stretching the dollar. One side benefit is this: that I have been able to empathize with those who are having to get along on a low income. And the chief benefit was this: I grew spiritually through coming

to know my Lord better. I found that godliness with contentment is great gain.

Someone has said that that person is greatly blessed who
can take money or leave it. The ideal is not to despise money
but to be master over it. Maturity in money matters is
achieved if you can admit with honest zest that you like
money (what it can buy), yet with the same zest know you
can get along without an abundance of money, if it's necessary.

In the days when we were experiencing financial stringencies, the writings of F. F. Bruce were not available to me.
But if I had had his expanded paraphrase, *The Letters of
Paul,* I would have been greatly helped by his rendering of
Philippians 4:11-13: "I have learned to be content in whatever condition I find myself. I know what it is to scrape the
bottom of the barrel; I know what it is to overflow. I have
passed through all the stages of initiation—fulness and hunger,
abundance and scarcity. I am able to meet them all, thanks
to my Enabler."[5]

Don't you like to hear Jesus Christ, the one who strengthens
us, described as our Enabler? I do.

The Amplified Bible gives a rendering of Philippians 4:13
which I like very much because it describes the kind of attitude I would like to have as I face the varying circumstances
of life: "I am ready for anything and equal to anything
through Him Who infuses inner strength into me, [that is, I
am self-sufficient in Christ's sufficiency]."

We do not come by such an attitude easily. It is learned.
As we look upon every situation in life as a learning experience, and trust in Jesus Christ as our Enabler, we shall
come to a mature faith which can be described as unquestion-
ing confidence in God.

And as the years go by and we look back upon God's dealings with us, we shall be able to say, as Paul did, "I thank
Christ Jesus our Lord, who hath enabled me" (1 Ti 1:12).

11

Tensions and Fatigue

In 1970 my husband and I had the privilege of participating in a family conference at a church in St. Louis. The first evening he talked to parents of teenage young people and I talked to parents of preteens. The next evening he talked to the men and I talked to the women about husband-wife relationships. These separate sessions were followed by a session for both husbands and wives in which they asked questions. The sessions were informal, with great freedom, and we had many laughs along with serious thinking on matters which are vital to a smoothly working marriage.

In my sessions with the women I talked about male and female differences, for I feel if women are aware of these, they won't be so puzzled about the behavior of their marriage partner and hence will be able to exercise more patience. (While preparing for this presentation I got valuable help from Cecil Osborne's *The Art of Understanding Your Mate.*[1])

A woman can be helped in understanding her husband when she recognizes that males in general are *doers* in contrast to women, who are *be-ers*. A man has more aggressive drive, which explains why males are the experimenters, explorers, directors and builders. A woman may have the ability to do many of the things men do which women don't ordinarily do, but she may not have the drive to do them. No one should assume that she is inferior because of this. She just finds her fulfillment in *being*—in being a person, a wife, a

71

mother, a keeper of spiritual values. Men, as leaders, take chances and run risks. Though women do less of this, they do have the innate capacity for leadership. Many have shown this in their management of a home and children when widowed—and sometimes a business which was formerly run by the husband.

The male produces the means of sustaining the family. This has been his traditional role. Now that so many women work, this role may be questioned. But many psychologists feel that even though the woman is employed and provides a second salary check for the family, the man should be the strong provider. For the sake of emphasizing the contrast, let me repeat: the male produces the means of sustaining the family; the female produces the children.

The husband's work is an extension of his personality. The wife's work at home is an extension of her personality. This is true even if she works outside her home, for her home has priority in her thinking.

The husband is more objective in his thinking, and relies on logic for understanding. The wife is more subjective and relies on intuition and "feelings" more than he.

To put it another way, men "externalize," and women "internalize." Men deal with facts, figures, general concepts, earning a living, and so on. Women get into things at the "feeling" level. Again, this does not mean the woman is inferior to man but rather that each is operating on a different wavelength.

To the male, the female is mysterious. But she shouldn't be viewed as mysterious so much as "different."

It's important for a minister's wife to be aware of such male-female differences because of their relation to tensions in husband-wife relationships. When she realizes that males generally possess these characteristics and sees how they affect his concept of himself, his work, and his home (and thus his priorities), then she can be more patient and understanding. Likewise, her awareness of woman's special ways of thinking and feeling will enable her to be more objective as she views herself.

She will not be able to live without *any* tensions, but she will be helped to live with them as she becomes aware of possible reasons for the inner tensions she may be experiencing.

I have already referred to some of the tensions a minister's wife may experience. I summarize them as follows:

1. Conflict between what is expected of her and what *she* wants to be and do.

2. Conflict between her concept of the "ideal" minister's wife and what she really is.

3. Feelings of inferiority because

   a. She didn't come from a home which provided her with a Christian background or a background of culture which would give her poise in entertaining and in situations where she needs to know the proper thing to do.

   b. She doesn't have a college education. Perhaps she worked while her husband completed his education. Now there is a culture gap between them.

   c. She doesn't have biblical knowledge to equip her for teaching a Bible class.

   d. She doesn't have natural gifts of leadership.

4. Feelings of discouragement because of

   a. Financial stringencies.

   b. Problems in the church.

   c. Criticism of her husband, her children, or herself.

5. Feelings of anxiety because of

   a. Present needs—making ends meet, as we say.

   b. Inability to save for future needs—for college funds for growing children, for a home, for retirement years.

Another source of anxiety feelings could be deep concern about her own health or her husband's health. For instance, some months ago I received a letter from a pastor's wife who said, "Last year my husband had a near-fatal illness. In our thirty-nine years of marriage he has never been seriously ill, and I guess I just counted on him as being indestructible and thought I would get to heaven first and not have to worry about a home, finances, and so on. Well, now some of those feelings are upon me, and the doctor says it is an anxiety neurosis and will go away in time. He has prescribed a very mild helpful tranquilizer in infant dosage. However, as a Christian I feel guilty taking these, and yet I say to myself, 'A diabetic takes insulin, and those with other ailments take the medications prescribed by their doctor.' "

This paragraph from my correspondent's letter points up another set of feelings a woman may have—feelings of guilt. I have received letters from women who are *not* pastors' wives who have expressed a similar guilt. They feel that because they are Christians they shouldn't need tranquilizers. Other women feel guilty about taking hormones prescribed by their doctor for certain symptoms some women have during the menopause. Some Christian women think they aren't "spiritual" when they get ill or when they have what is called a "nervous breakdown."

Of course, we may fail (and this is particularly true of ministers' wives) in making wise decisions in allocating priorities. Or we may become tired just thinking of all the things we have to do—not only things *we* expect of ourselves but also things others expect of us. For instance, a minister's wife who corresponded with me during the summer lull in their church's schedule of activities said, "I will not be able to hear you often on radio because all the meetings start again in another week or so. I counted twenty-one meetings per month which I attend, in addition to invitational affairs." And then she told me about her frequent crying spells.

Sometimes a woman needs to shape her lips to say very firmly a two-letter word spelled N-O. But many a minister's wife feels she shouldn't say no to anything connected with the work of the church her husband pastors, and she feels guilty if she does.

To help you in evaluating the problem of fatigue which may in turn enable you to avoid a feeling of guilt, I quote some material on the subject of fatigue which I found in Dr. Marion Nelson's book *Why Christians Crack Up*. Dr. Nelson is a physician specializing in the field of psychiatry, and his background includes several years of theological training. Dr. Nelson says:

> Fatigue, when it develops, prevents the mind from being as efficient or as effective (as it might be) in coping with problems. A person who is fatigued may also be nervous and irritable. If a person works all day and fails to get enough relaxation or sleep, he will develop fatigue sooner or later. This fatigue may lead to some type of breakdown unless a proper balance of work, sleep and relaxation is restored.
>
> This is easy to see in the young housewife and mother who perhaps has had her third baby and now finds herself going around all day minding babies, fixing bottles, handling diapers, washing and ironing, doing housework, cooking meals and losing sleep at night. Her life frequently becomes unbalanced with too much work and not enough relaxation and rest. She tries to accomplish more and more work in one day's time, doing too many things too quickly, living under constant pressure, and then finds herself feeling tired. She is developing fatigue.
>
> She goes to the doctor complaining of being tired and perhaps nervous. The doctor examines her, does a blood count, maybe checks her metabolism, and ends up finding no organic disease.
>
> She is suffering from chronic fatigue, which makes her mind as well as her body feel tired. A tired mind cannot cope with the problems of everyday living effectively, and so she becomes irritated by minor things that ordinarily would not irritate her.

She loses her enthusiasm for the things she used to enjoy. She doesn't seem to feel the same love toward her husband. She develops a carelessness toward things about which she should be careful. She doesn't seem to think about God as much any more, or read the Bible and pray as she used to. She asks, "Am I backslidden?" The answer is probably no. She is not backslidden; she is fatigued, and this has affected her mind. It is obvious that this same process is going on in many businessmen today who allow the pressures of business to crowd them into a daily schedule that is entirely too busy.

Remember that God the Holy Spirit, in speaking to us as Christians, works through our conscious mind. If our mind is fatigued and befuddled, then the Holy Spirit cannot get through to us as well as before. We cannot pray as we used to do because prayer is an exercise of the mind, and if the mind is tired, naturally we cannot pray as well.

. . . There is a limit of stamina, which varies with individuals; exceeding this limit puts a definite strain upon both the body and the mind. The body and mind carry this burdensome load for a time, but eventually, if the person does not slow down and relax, the body and mind develop fatigue, which forces the person to slow down. If he takes the hint conveyed to him by fatigue and rests and relaxes more at this point, then the fatigue will disappear after a while.

If he ignores the warning symptom of fatigue, then eventually he will reach a point where his body and mind simply refuse to go on at that fast pace. At this point he may have what is commonly called a nervous breakdown (which is a somewhat vague term but yet one which everyone seems to recognize). At any rate, the body and mind refuse to carry the burden any longer, and the person has to take a rest and get out from under the pressure because he becomes physically and mentally incapacitated.

Of course, when this happens, rest is just what he needs. After he has rested a while he begins to improve. For a while he will continue to reap the results of the abnormal strain pressed upon himself, but in time the reaping process

comes to an end and he gets well. This process of improve-
ment usually takes place in some hospital or rest home or
at his own home, where he is forced to do nothing but rest
and relax, whereas he should have been resting properly in
a balanced life all along, as a preventative measure.

The Lord Jesus Christ had to take time out occasionally
to rest during His ministry here upon the earth, because
He was truly human. As a man He felt the need of periodic
rest and relaxation, away from the crowds of people to
whom He ministered (Mark 6:31).

Sometimes, however, a person cannot avoid a time of
heavy work and pressure. A college student, for example, . . .
should be careful to follow each school period of work
and study and pressure with a period of less work and more
rest, to help him build up resistance against fatigue. A period
of abnormally heavy strain ought to be followed by a period
of unusually light strain. This will enable his body and mind
to recover, and thus he can avoid a breakdown.

A breakdown results when there has been too much strain,
and pressure for too long a time, without enough rest. One
cannot ignore God's laws of nature regarding the needs of
our body and mind for rest and relaxation.

. . . The development of fatigue is usually an indication
that the Christian has been trying to do more work than God
has willed for him to do in that period of time. If you cannot work sixteen hours a day without developing fatigue,
then it is very unlikely that God would lead you to work
sixteen hours a day. When God's sustaining grace expires
for that day and you become tired, then it is time to quit
and rest instead of continuing your labor.

God does not lead Christians to abuse their bodies and
minds with too much work. God wants us to take proper
care of our bodies and minds as well as we know how. For
it is through us, our bodies and minds, the vessels of God,
that God works. If our mind is numb with fatigue, we are
not capable of being used effectively by the Holy Spirit. So in
regard to this factor of fatigue, the best thing to do is to

avoid overwork by living a balanced life. If fatigue develops because of overwork, then the cure is to get more rest and relaxation.[2]

Then Dr. Nelson added a warning to the effect that the Christian who lets himself become fatigued is asking for trouble. Because the fatigued Christian is not alert and on guard as he should be, he offers Satan an ideal opportunity to launch an attack. Christians always need to be in the best condition possible for serving the Lord and for warding off Satan's attacks.

Apropos to the discussion of the subject of fatigue is a paragraph which I found in a book about the power of Christian love, *And the Greatest of These,* by George Sweeting:

> I once heard of an artist who was commissioned to design a trademark. After some time he submitted his design and a bill for $500. The design was unusually simple, and the client questioned the artist on the steep price. The artist answered, "The charge is for knowing what to leave out." In the business of everyday living, it is important to know what to leave out. There are so many things to absorb us, to use up our time and our energies. We must learn to leave out the trivialities and concentrate on the essentials.[3]

And I would add, we must learn to do it without being burdened with a sense of guilt. Keep in mind that it's no sin to get tired, but it is a sin to let tiredness get the best of you.

12

Priorities

The Tyranny of the Urgent is the intriguing title of a booklet by Charles Hummel that attracted my attention on a day when I was browsing in a bookstore. I purchased it, and soon after started to read it. But I didn't finish it until months later. Since the booklet contained only fifteen pages, what was the reason for my delay in finishing the booklet? The tyranny of the urgent.

Our lives are made up of innumerable situations like that. There are so many worthwhile things we want to do and don't do—or begin to do and lay aside—because something urgent demands our time and attention.

Feeding and clothing our children are two of the urgencies of life. However, it is important that we give them our presence, attention, and active love.

Eating nourishing, well-balanced meals to strengthen our bodies is urgent. However, it is important that we nourish our minds through learning and reading, and it's important that we nourish our spiritual natures. Jesus said, "Man shall not live by bread alone, but by every word that proceedeth out of the mouth of God" (Mt 4:4).

Success in one's vocation is urgent. But it is important that we also achieve success in the art of real living. Jesus said, "I am come that they [His sheep, those who know Him and follow Him] might have life, and . . . have it more abundantly" (Jn 10:10). We can succeed in the art of real living,

abundant living, only as we make use of the spiritual resources God has made available to believers in His Son.

It's entirely possible for us to allow "thieves" to rob us of
abundant living by yielding to urgent demands on our time,
energy and attention. To avoid this we will need to make
distinctions between what is urgent and what is important. In
other words, we need to exercise discernment for setting
priorities in our lives. We will need to be selective.

In the life of a minister's wife, what others expect of her
may appear to be urgent. She is reluctant to say no to any
request. Why? Because she feels she must always appear as
the gracious, adaptable, self-sacrificial person who measures
up to her concept of the ideal minister's wife.

Many times the need of her children for her presence is
more important than a church meeting. I remember a night
when I felt that I ought to attend a meeting of an organization
in our church known as The Missionary Helpers. At this
meeting we gained information about the missionaries in
whose financial support our church shared, we prayed for
them, and sewed for them or planned for purchases of items
which they needed. Well, that night my husband couldn't stay
home with our youngest son, and my two older boys (then
of high school age) had commitments. I was unsuccessful in
my efforts to get a sitter to stay with Mark, so I reluctantly
stayed home with him. I sat with him as he practiced his
piano lesson, and after that we went upstairs where he readied
himself for bed. Then we kneeled to pray by his bedside.
When we arose, I was about to begin reading a Bible story to
him. But I noticed that his eyes were filled with tears, and I
heard him saying, "Mother, I want to be a Christian." I had
assumed that he was a Christian since he had told me when
he was about six years old, in answer to my questions, that he
loved Jesus and had let Him come into his life. Now, at age
ten, he was considering his relationship to the Lord Jesus in
a more mature way. How glad I was that circumstances had

compelled me to remain at home with him that night. The missionary meeting had seemed to be urgent, but being with my son was important.

Many times a minister's wife will recognize that it is more important for her to take time for Bible study than to yield to the urgency of household tasks not completed. And it may seem that those tasks are screaming at her when she sits down to study the Bible for an hour or so. But she can mentally tune them out, knowing that they will be waiting for her when she leaves her "inner sanctuary with the Lord" to return to whatever awaits her attention. And she will carry with her the inspiration and uplift of that time spent alone with the Lord and with His Word. I find that I often work more efficiently and with a happier spirit after my inner man has been refreshed by drinking at the spring of "living waters."

In the years when our boys were growing up and I was carrying a heavy load of activities in our church, I came to realize that I couldn't be a perfect housekeeper and also be prepared to do the Bible teaching I wanted to, conduct children's meetings, and attend prayer meetings and women's meetings. Now I see that if I had not continued the Bible teaching and the study required to prepare for the classes I taught, I wouldn't have been ready for the radio ministry into which the Lord has led me and in which I have been engaged since 1959.

At times a minister's wife may decide that it is more important for her to get some extra rest and relaxation, to avoid becoming absolutely exhausted, instead of yielding to urgent invitations of officers of various church organizations to be present at their meetings. But when she doesn't attend and feels she is neglecting church work, her conscience may torment her, placing upon her a burden of guilt. However, if she can learn to make a distinction between what is urgent and what is important, she may rise above the tendency to feel guilty.

We who are ministers' wives need to balance our roles, and this entails facing the fact that we cannot fill all of them perfectly. As we seek to balance our roles we will need to be selective in the use of our time and energy.

To exercise discernment in making choices is one of the marks of maturity. Hebrews 5:12-14 is on the subject of maturity. In that section of Scripture we read about individuals who, in view of the length of time they had been Christians, should have been teachers of the truth of God but were then in need of being fed with milk. That is, they needed to be taught again the ABC's of the gospel. Those who had not remained in spiritual babyhood but had gone on to maturity were described as full-grown. They could feed on the "strong meat" of God's Word, and were described as persons who "by reason of use" had "their senses exercised to discern both good and evil."

Kenneth Wuest in his *Expanded Translation of the New Testament* translates this verse this way: "Solid food belongs to those who are [spiritually] mature, to those who on account of long usage have their powers of perception exercised to the point where they are able to discriminate between both that which is good in character and that which is evil."[1]

I often say, when speaking to audiences of Christian women, "Most of you do not need to use your ability to discern in making distinctions between good and evil as much as you need to use this ability in choosing between the good, the better, and the best. Often the *good* is the enemy of the *best*."

I wonder if, in the busyness of your life, you have ever felt like this:

> From morning until night
> I am busy.
> Surely all this motion
> is getting me somewhere,
> isn't it?

Somewhere . . .
What an indefinite term!
Where am I going?
Am I any closer to being there
than I was yesterday?
I don't know . . .
I've been so busy going,
I haven't thought about
where . . .
Of course, I know
I want to know God,
Now . . .
as He is revealed in Jesus Christ.
Let's check and see if I'm going
ahead,
or backward,
or nowhere . . .[2]

I hope that you will check on yourself and that your daily choices will result in your coming to know God better and better and thus becoming more like Him. Second Corinthians 3:18 says that those who with unveiled (or uncovered) face look into the mirror of the Word of God are changed into the same image (the image of Him who is the living Word, Jesus Christ) from glory unto glory.

As you make progress in becoming like Him, you will be making progress along the road to maturity.

13

A Time Study

Years ago I read on a church offering envelope a statement that has stayed with me, and which I often recall: "The President of the United States has twenty-four hours in his day, and so do you."

And I thought, *That's true. But he has numerous assistants, and I don't.* As I continued to think about the statement, I recognized that he deserved all those assistants because of the vast scope of his responsibilities.

However, I have often wished I could stretch my daily allotment of twenty-four hours into thirty-six. But I can't. The clocks in my home run at the same rate as those in the homes of my neighbors. There are only sixty minutes in each hour available to me. This is true for every living person.

Even though I can't stretch time, I can learn how to manage better in the time I have.

There are many confusing thoughts about time. And since time affects each of us every day of our lives, I want to share with you some thoughts on the subject which I gleaned from a chapter titled "What Is Time?" in a book authored by Ted W. Engstrom and Alec Mackenzie, *Managing Your Time.*

The chapter began with a quotation from an ancient source—Saint Augustine, who lived from A.D. 354 to 430. He said, "What is Time? Who is able easily and briefly to explain it? Who is able so much as in thought to comprehend it so as to express himself concerning it? And yet what in our usual discourse do we more familiarly and knowingly make more mention of than Time? And surely we understand it well enough when we speak of it; we understand it also when in speaking with another we hear it named. What then is Time? If nobody asks me I know; but if I were desirous to explain it to someone that should ask me, plainly I know not."

Henry Austin Dobson, who lived fifteen hundred years later, penned two lines which capture part of the confusion about time:

> Time goes, you say? Ah, no!
> Alas, Time stays, we go.

Robert M. MacIver, Lieber Professor of Political Philosophy and Sociology at Columbia University from 1927 to 1950, concluded that time, like space, is a dimension rather than a force.

Now that I have shared with you these references to time by three men who lived in widely separated periods of history, references which I found in the book *Managing Your Time,* I quote from this book the following paragraphs which point up some misconceptions about time:

> In the lives of busy executives there is no question asked more often than "Where has the time gone?" Does it seem strange that the question most often asked, rhetorically to be sure, should so misstate the case? Does time depart the scene as the question suggests? Or has it simply passed at the rate it always has while we accomplished far less than we should? Or, perhaps, are we really asking, "How could I have planned so poorly and have left so much to be done in so little time?"
>
> "Time is money and must be spent wisely," we have been told all our lives. But have we any choice *not* to spend it? Of course we do not. The hands of the clock move onward inexorably. We have no control over the speed of their progress. We may "stop the clock" on a basketball court or on a football field—but never in the game of life.
>
> The sundial's shadow and the sands in the hourglass mean something more than a commodity to be controlled or dis-

pensed at will. So we speak of the ravages of time . . . a
hand that cannot be stayed . . . a scythe with which an old
man levels all. But is time really a force to be so dreaded,
or does it in fact create nothing . . . destroy nothing?

Faith Baldwin called time a seamstress specializing in al-
terations. But we know that rocks wear down and stars grow
dim, men age and empires decay, *not* because time works on
them but because of the ebb and flow of energy systems
operating within the physical laws of the universe established
by God. If space is the dimension in which things exist, why
not accept time, as Dr. Robert MacIver suggests, as the
dimension in which things change?

"Time flies!" we exclaim—when we mean that we have
not accomplished the results expected within the time available.

"Time will take care of it," we say—instead of asserting
that the condition will undoubtedly rectify itself, given adequate time.

"I don't have the time," we protest—instead of admitting
that the proposal is not sufficiently important in our priorities to warrant *taking* the time for it. We always make time
for things that are important enough.

We talk about the "tyranny of time," ascribing to it a
capability of acting instead of recognizing it as a measurement of too large a number of tasks to be performed within
the time available.

After all, time isn't money or even a commodity; it's not
going anywhere . . . can't be speeded up or slowed down; it
can't be bought or bartered; it's not a ravaging force of evil
or an inscrutable judge or an omniscient healer. Time is, as
Webster put it simply, "the period during which action or
process continues." Like sands in the hourglass, so are the
days of our lives.[1]

So, as we consider the work God has given us to do and
evaluate the resources He has granted us for our task, we
come to the conclusion that a fixed amount of time is available for us to use. And we find in the Bible, in Colossians

4:5, an injunction to Christians of the first century about their use of time—an injunction which we can apply to ourselves: "Be wise in your behavior toward non-Christians, and make the best possible use of your time" (Phillips).

We might think of time as a stewardship, just as we view money and possessions and talents as stewardships for which we are accountable to God. We are stewards of our time.

> What do we mean by referring to ourselves as "stewards of our time"? Is it really *our* time we're talking about, or is it *God's* time? Has it been granted to us, along with the gift of life itself, to be disposed according to our purposes . . . with only a portion of our own determination going back to Him from when it came? Or, . . . since God fashioned the world and all that is in it, does *all* our time *belong to Him?*[2]

If you give a positive answer to that question, time becomes—for you—management of God's time. Such an answer leads you to another question: "Am I doing what *God* wants me to do within the dimension of time He has given me?"

Since one characteristic of the mature Christian is the ability to discern, to make the right choices, some of us who consider ourselves to be mature may well question our maturity if we are failing to make wise choices about what God wants us to be doing. Really, the problem comes down to this: Since God has promised to supply my every need and already has supplied my need of time to do the things I ought to do, the solution to the problem of better management of time can be arrived at by giving an answer to this question: Am I in the center of God's will for my life?

To be in the center of God's will for your life implies managing yourself, disciplining yourself to say no to those activities which are not within God's will for you, and to say yes to what you are persuaded is God's will for you this day. You have only today. Yesterday is past, and tomorrow is not here.

14

Stress and Strain

The stresses and strains we experience in life are described in various ways: as tensions, pressures, testings, problems.

As I was preparing for a talk to a group of ministers' wives a few years ago on the subject of "The Tensions of the Pastor's Wife," I looked up the word *tension* in Webster's unabridged dictionary. You can be quite confident that you know what a word means until you are asked to give a definition. Even Saint Augustine said he would have felt this way if he were asked to explain what time is, as indicated by his writing, "What then is time? If nobody asks me I know; but if I were desirous to explain it to someone that should ask me, plainly I know not."

What did I discover about tension by referring to the dictionary? I found several definitions. The first was this: "The act of stretching, straining, or tensing; a state or degree of being stretched or strained to stiffness, as seen in tension of the muscles." Hence, tension could refer to mental strain and intensity of feeling or effort; nervous discontent or anxiety; and strained condition of relationship as between nations, individuals, or groups.

I also found that *tension* could be used medically in references to strain or pressure, as arterial tension; the feeling of muscular tension or expectancy; unrest and striving due to inner physiological causes. These medical definitions refer to conditions that can be caused by attitudes, fears or challenges.

I discovered, too, a mechanical definition of tension: "A force (either of two balancing forces) causing or tending to cause extension." Examples of the use of such force are a bridge which is designed to bear the stress of estimated loads and certain wind forces, and skyscrapers which are planned by architects and engineers to bear certain loads and even to take the stress of high winds.

As I considered the mechanical definition of tension, I couldn't help but think, *God is wiser than any engineer or architect, and He knows how much stress and strain we can take.*

Not only is God wise in His dealings with us; He is concerned about us as persons. From 1 Corinthians 10:13 we learn that God will not allow us to be tempted (or tested) above that which we are able to bear. He doesn't exempt us from the stresses and strains of life. Like a skyscraper we may have to feel the brunt of winds that test the product of the knowledge and skill of its designers. We, too, can "take it." Since God has made us, He knows what "makes us tick" and what we can take in the way of trials. It's encouraging for us who are Christians to know that we have more resources for meeting the stresses and strains of life than do those persons who are not Christians. Some Christians fail to make use of those resources and consequently suffer discouragement and defeat. But those who rely on the indwelling Spirit for the strength He supplies to those who trust Him for that purpose will be able to take the tensions of life without breaking.

Tension isn't always bad or harmful. Anyone who performs in public by singing, playing an instrument, or giving a speech is under tension to some degree. Anyone who performs as an athlete knows what tension is. When my eldest son played basketball in high school and college, he would frequently say before a game, "I have butterflies in my stomach." That was a sign of tension. From what I have heard, coaches don't want their players fully relaxed because a certain amount of tension is normal when an athlete is engaged in competition.

The apostle Paul used figures of speech which were familiar to those who watched the Grecian games in the stadia of his day. He said of himself, "I press toward the mark for the prize of the high calling of God" (Phil 3:14). He also said, "Those who run in a race all run, but only one receives the prize" (1 Co 9:24, NASB).

The writer of the epistle to the Hebrews wrote: "Let us lay aside every weight . . . and run with patience the race [the course] that is set before us" (12:1), and in the next verse he referred to Jesus, "Who, for the joy set before Him endured the cross."

We can endure the unpleasant and even painful present experiences if we have faith and confidence in what God has said about what the future holds for those who endure. We who are God's children can endure because of our relationship with a world of eternal values through our living relationship with Jesus Christ and because of the spiritual resources God has made available to us. For this reason, because we believe our working through our difficult situations will yield benefits both for this life and for the life beyond this earthly life—not only for ourselves but for others—we can endure.

The apostle James gave an admonition about trials that you may have found difficult to accept: "Count it all joy, my brethren, when ye fall into manifold temptations [or testings]" (1:2, ASV). It's natural for us to count it joy when we avoid testings, isn't it? The paraphrase of the New Testament known as the Living New Testament is very down-to-earth in its rendering of this verse and its context: "Dear brothers, is your life full of difficulties and temptations? Then be happy. For when the way is rough, your patience has a chance to grow. So let it grow, and don't try to squirm out of your problems. For when your patience is finally in full bloom, then you will be ready for anything, strong in character, full and complete" (Ja 1:2-4).

In my opinion, "strong in character, full and complete" describes spiritual maturity. But such maturity is only achieved through growth. "When the way is rough, your patience has a chance to grow. So let it grow, and don't try to squirm out of your problems" (Living NT). So, meet your problems, your tensions, your pressures, as challenges to faith and count on God to see you through. As you do, you will grow and mature.

Looking back on my life, I can see how I have grown and matured through the experiences of being a wife and mother —and a pastor's wife. I learned much through the experiences of those years.

And by having to extend myself since I was widowed in 1961, I have grown and matured. I had to learn to live alone, to stand on my own two feet financially. I said yes to the invitation to write and produce a five-times-a-week radio program, "Woman to Woman." I had no preparation for work in radio except as God had prepared me through my knowledge of Him and of His Word, and what I had learned from Him through the various circumstances of life. These included learning to adapt to my husband, to motherhood, to persons in the churches my husband pastored, to financial stringencies as the inflation spiral ascended faster than the increases in my husband's salary, to the criticisms I heard of my children when my sons didn't always, during their teen years, perfectly fulfill our expectations or those of some of our parishioners. I also learned some lessons through sickness and sorrow.

And yet, after I had accepted the invitation to this radio ministry, I went through a period of uncertainty. Should I continue, or should I accept other offers of positions that would offer me more economic security? This inner dialogue continued for about five months. I was extremely tired during those months, for the emotional tension caused by inability to come to a decision can be exhausting. But one night, which was typical of many others when I would awaken and be unable to go back to sleep because of this inner dialogue, a portion of 2 Corinthians 2:16 came to mind without any conscious effort on my part. It came to me as a personal question related to my situation: "Who is sufficient for these things?" Immediately, again without any conscious effort on my part, came an answer to the question from the next chapter: "Our sufficiency is of God" (2 Co 3:5).

Since that night I have not doubted what God wanted me to do. And I have been able to apply to myself these words from Philippians 4:13, "I can do all things through Christ which strengtheneth me." And the rendering of this verse in the Amplified Bible has come to mean very much to me: "I am ready for anything and equal to anything through Him Who infuses inner strength into me, [that is, I am self-sufficient in Christ's sufficiency]."

 You who have been called to fill the role of minister's wife can be sure that you will be sufficient (or adequate) for your role as you rely on Christ's sufficiency.

15

Anxiety or Trust?

I wonder if you have reacted to statements you have read or heard about ministers' wives suffering nervous breakdowns by saying something like this: "Some of those ministers' wives might have had breakdowns even if they hadn't been married to a clergyman!" Granted! But if such a woman were not in the position of minister's wife with its consequent relationship to her husband's congregation with all their expectations of her and her family, she might have been able to cope with her tensions with a little more ease because she could have "let down" more than she was able to as the wife of a minister.

One of the churches of which my first husband was pastor hosted the board members of a mission society and candidates for service under the auspices of the society. Among the candidates were two physicians, and during their free time one afternoon I took them on a tour of the church facilities. One of the doctors asked me, "How do you like being a minister's wife?" I replied, "Fine. But you can never let down."

I guess I was thinking of that phase of the life of a minister's wife which might be considered "public relations." You are always conscious of impressions being made and of their effect on your husband's ministry and the church he pastors. Even though I concede that wives of men in public life in positions other than the ministry may be conscious of the "public relations" aspect of their lives, I think the wife of a minister is under extra pressure because of this aspect of her life. And if the descriptions I have read about the kind of women (ministers' wives) who have breakdowns is correct, then this extra pressure is just enough to tip the scales toward a breakdown. These women are described as conscientious women who are unable to meet adequately all the demands made on them as they take on the responsibilities of a minister's wife.

Contributing to the problem of such a woman is the busyness of her husband's life. However, if she is in love with her husband she wants to have him spend more time with her than he does. But he is conscientious too, and feels he must make all those home calls on the sick and shut-ins and on those who are hospitalized. And when he is asked to perform wedding ceremonies and conduct funerals, he cannot turn down these requests.

Then there are those parishioners who need counseling (or think they do). Counseling takes much of the minister's time —and sometimes the time of the minister's wife. If she is overly conscientious she may have feelings of guilt because she can do so little to help people with their problems. One minister's wife said in a letter to me, "Each day our walls echo with the problems of our beloved people—problems of sickness and death, young people's problems, and so on. Somehow I want to *do* something about everybody, and that is impossible. To *pray* for them is all that I can do—and no less than that. Sometimes I feel so guilty when some good soul calls and says, 'Just to hear your voice calms me,' and I think, *What a double life I lead!"*

This woman has been troubled with what her doctor calls an anxiety neurosis, and for this the doctor has prescribed a mild tranquilizer. But she feels guilty about taking a tranquilizer. In her letter she asked this question: "Why can't I trust the Lord completely with my life just as my two-year-old granddaughter trusts me as she curls up in my arms?"

Another pastor's wife was troubled because of her inability to keep to a schedule which she had planned for her household tasks. She said, "Our boys are 7, 6, 5, and 1½ years old. . . . A steady stream of visitors continually comes to our house. As you know from your experience as a pastor's wife, this doesn't help in keeping a schedule nor does it contribute to the tranquillity of our home." I told her, "While it's wise to make out a schedule, you need to prepare yourself for interruptions and changes of plans for a particular day. Flexibility is the key word."

One mother (not a pastor's wife) said in discussing this very problem, "You need to learn to bend with the wind." The branch that is rigid and inflexible will break with the wind. What she said brought to my mind something I hadn't thought of for years: a description of a painting of a storm in which the sky was filled with dark clouds. You could tell there was a strong wind because the artist had painted trees bending under the force of the wind. The focal point of the picture, in a nest in the foreground, was a bird which appeared to be singing.

Surely we to whom God has given intelligence whereby we can comprehend what He has said about Himself (His love, His power, His wisdom, His concern for us, His steadfast mercy) should be able to trust Him more intelligently than the bird pictured by the artist, more intelligently than the two-year-old baby resting in her grandmother's lap. *They* do it by intuition; *we* should do it with intelligence. We have been given in God's Word all that we need to know in order to trust Him. Jesus said, using the illustration of God's care for sparrows, "Not one of them falls to the ground without your heavenly Father's knowledge," which would mean, of course, without His allowing it. And then Jesus added this comment, "Fear ye not therefore, ye are of more value than many sparrows." Our value is demonstrated by the fact that God gave His well-beloved Son to die for us, and that He sent His Holy Spirit to live in our hearts to strengthen us, to guide us, to teach us, to enable us to be the kind of persons He wants us to be.

Jesus, in talking to His disciples about worry, impressed upon them that their anxiety (taking thought for the morrow) would not enable any one of them to add one cubit to his stature, or, as suggested by Kenneth Taylor's paraphrase in the Living New Testament, their "worries" would not "add a single moment" to their life.

It's fine for a pastor's wife to be concerned about the problems in their congregation, but she cannot carry their problems like a burden. With their problems as well as her own, she must do what the apostle Peter advised the early Christians to do. He told them to cast all their cares upon the Lord, and assured them of God's ever continuing care.

Yes, God cares for you, and He cares for the persons about whom you are concerned. His concern for them is even greater than your concern, and He ever lives to make intercession for those who come to God by Him.

It's easy, since the world is so full of needs, to feel at a loss when you consider the magnitude of those needs. You want to do something about them, but you know that what you can do is limited. I like what was said by a Chinese woman, a pediatrician who could have served usefully in many places— in her homeland, on various mission fields, but who stayed in New York City. She said, "The needs are many and great, and I am only one person. But what I *can* do I *will* do, by the grace of God."

Anyone who takes such an attitude and follows through with appropriate action can do one more thing: Ask the Lord to lay some of the needs of the world upon the hearts of other individuals who will say, "I am only one, but what I *can* do I *will* do, with God's help."

Faith is our response to what God has said. This response consists of attitude (confidence in God) and action (doing what He wants us to do). During one of my perusals of chapter 11 of Hebrews, I was struck by the repeated use of the two words "by faith." And as I considered what these words implied in the experiences of the people listed in this chapter, I saw that having faith doesn't always mean expecting miracles. Most of the time it means maintaining confidence in God. The practicality of faith is shown in the following instances:

By faith Enoch walked with God, and pleased Him.

By faith Moses endured. *Endurance* is another word for *patience*. (I would like to interject two brief descriptions of patience which I came across in my reading: "Patience is faith in the *long* run." "Patience is the ability to care slowly." I think pastors' wives and all mothers need that kind of patience.)

By faith Moses made the right choices. By faith we can receive from God wisdom for making right choices day by day.

By faith some of God's people were able, out of weakness, to be made strong. They "were made strong again after they had been weak or sick" (Heb 11:34, Living NT).

By faith some of God's servants obtained God's approval (v.39). And we can, too, as we walk by faith, which means living by faith, living in dependence upon God, relying upon the strength and wisdom He will give us, expecting Him to work in situations where we can do nothing; that is, nothing but pray and wait for Him to work.

16

"I Need Someone to Talk to and to Listen to Me!"

Knowing about possible causes for tensions, and knowing about the differences in male and female characteristics is one thing. Knowing how to apply such knowledge to your situation is another. This was brought sharply to my attention in a discussion group following presentations my husband and I had made at a family life conference in a church in the St. Louis area. A young woman rose to her feet and said, "Well, I'm glad to know all that, but what do I *do* about a husband who won't communicate, who won't talk with me and listen to me? And what do I do about myself, when I'm ready to *explode* because I need to talk with someone about how I feel inside?"

I imagine many a minister's wife has felt that way at times. Sometimes a husband and wife can talk with others and counsel with others, but they don't talk to each other about their problems. When this is the case, they are neglecting one of the simple ways of relieving tensions: talking them out with someone else. Of course, we Christians know that we can talk over any problem, any of our tensions, with God. We can tell Him everything that is on our hearts, knowing that He will understand. Because we know His heart is full of loving concern for us, we can be sure He will give us aid.

But if I were to tell you only that, and advise you to pray about your tensions, I would be like the mother of the girl who appeared as a missionary candidate before the home missions board of which I was a member for six years. Telling of experiences in her youth, she said that her mother would say to her when she went to her with a problem, "Pray about it." This girl said, "I knew that. I knew I could pray to God about it. I wanted my mother to *listen* to me, and to talk with me about my problem."

And that's the way many of us often feel. As someone has expressed it, "We want to talk to someone with skin on."

The Bible recognizes the benefit of counseling with others. In a number of places in the book of Proverbs the value of receiving counsel from others is stressed. Of course, before giving counsel the counselor must first *listen* to your problem.

Proverbs 11:14: "Where no counsel is, the people fall; but in the multitude of counsellors there is safety."

Proverbs 12:15: "The way of a fool is right in his own eyes: but he that hearkeneth unto counsel is wise."

Proverbs 15:22: "Without counsel purposes are disappointed: but in the multitude of counsellors they are established."

Proverbs 19:20: "Hear counsel, and receive instruction, that thou mayest be wise in thy latter end."

Proverbs 19:21: "There are many devices in a man's heart; nevertheless the counsel of the LORD, that shall stand."

Proverbs 20:18: "Every purpose is established by counsel."

In the New Testament the value of mutual confession and mutual encouragement is taught. In James 5 are these words: "Confess your faults one to another, and pray one for another." Hebrews 10:24-25 presents this exhortation: "Let us consider one another to provoke unto love and to good works: not forsaking the assembling of ourselves together." The value of Christian friends for spiritual strengthening and encouragement is seen again and again in the book of Acts and the epistles of the New Testament.

But so often the minister's wife and the minister feel that they cannot open their hearts to their people and freely talk about their tensions, their discouragements, their self-doubts, because they feel it would weaken their ministry among their people. It seems that people assume that the minister and his wife are different than they are, so the minister and his wife, even though they have many friends in their congregation, lead a sort of lonely existence. Some of them find other couples in the ministry with whom they can visit and talk over problems and with whom they can pray. Other young ministerial couples have told how they have been helped by periods of fellowship with a couple in the ministry who are older than they and who tell what they have learned from their own experience.

Ideally, a pastor and his wife should be able to communicate, to share, to be honest and open with each other. Too many times, though, a pastor has spent so much time counseling others that he is tired of listening to problems, and when he comes home he wants to forget about problems. But this is hard on his wife and family.

Joseph T. Bayly in his monthly feature in *Eternity* magazine told of a minister friend who was deeply concerned when two of his three sons began to stutter. This minister made an appointment for them to see a speech therapist who was also a psychologist, and later had a conference himself. The minister related, "That psychologist literally cursed me. He told me I was responsible for that speech defect, and that I was ruining my boys' lives. He asked me, 'When did you last take your family on a vacation?' "

In talking with Mr. Bayly, the minister said, "Well, it had been a long, long time. I was too busy to take *time* with my family. I remember that I used to say that the Devil never takes a vacation, so why should I? And I never stopped to think that the *Devil* wasn't to be my *example*. I went out of that man's office, got a camping trailer, and in a few days we were headed West. The second day out my wife nudged me, and I listened to the conversation on the back seat. There wasn't a trace of a speech defect from those boys. I pulled over to the side of the road and bawled like a baby."[1]

That is an unusual case, in my opinion. However, it points up that small boys feel terribly neglected if their father has no time for them.

And some ministers' wives feel that way. I remember reading in *Moody Monthly* magazine a few years ago about a woman who was described as the forgotten wife of a Christian worker. The editors received a flood of letters from readers giving advice. While many were sympathetic with the problem of a minister who is so busy that he has little time for his family, most of them seemed to feel that the wife should be able to feed her own inner spiritual life. One woman said, "What if God took your husband away from you? Then who would you turn to? The Lord, of course. Then why not trust Him now? He is our burden bearer."

Another said, "She should turn directly to the Lord. If she should depend on her husband or anyone else, she will ever remain a spiritual dwarf."

I agree that spiritual growth is essential not only for a minister's wife but for all Christians. However, we need to face the fact that in marriage we cannot neglect one another. As persons who are significant to each other, we need to nourish this relationship of love and caring by periods when we can give our undivided attention to each other.

One wife of a pastor told a group of ministers' wives at a retreat where I spoke that she let her husband know she wanted time with him by blocking out a space of time for herself in his appointment book so that they could go out to dinner together. Or she blocked out a space of time for the family to go on an outing of some kind.

Though the following conversation is fiction (the product of Edna Gerstner's imagination), I use it to illustrate the subject I have been discussing. The dialog is between John Calvin and his wife. Calvin, noted French Protestant Reformer, was living in Strasbourg when he married Idelette de

Bure in 1540. In 1541 they moved to Geneva, where he spent the rest of his days. A scholar, he spent a great deal of time studying and writing, and may have become so engrossed in his labors that he spent little time with his wife.

They strolled together by the blue lake, pausing to feed the swans. And Genevan eyebrows lifted and friends smiled to see Jean Calvin pleasure-walking with his wife.

"Are you enjoying yourself?" Idelette asked anxiously.

"Very much. And you?"

"My conscience troubles me," said his wife.

"Why?"

"I am burdened with the feeling I am keeping you from God's work."

"This is God's work." Then seeing the bewilderment on his wife's face he explained, "It is a husband's duty to spend time with his wife and family."

"Beware! I shall hold you to those words."

"You threaten!"

"I do."

He smiled down at her, "So little and so frightening a wife I have chosen." He crumbled a piece of bread for a gull and threw it in the air. The swift bird swooped down and caught the fragment in mid-air. "Do I neglect you, Idelette?"

"Why do you ask?"

"That is no answer."

"If you ever do I know it is for God's work. I would not have it otherwise."

"You are a good wife."

Idelette was pleased with his rare praise. "But why, Jean, why all these questions?"

"I have been very severely scolded today for my neglect of you."

"How dare anyone interfere in what is our private affair?"

"This one has every right."

"Who spoke to you about the matter?"

"God."

"What did He say?"

"He spoke as always through His revealed will. I was reading the first epistle of Corinthians, the seventh chapter, and the third verse, *'Que le mari rende á sa femme la bienveillance.'* Let the man render unto his wife true friendship.' "

"And what did you reply?"

"I said, 'I will.' "

And so it became no longer an uncommon sight to see Monsieur and Madame Calvin strolling together of an evening. For God had spoken.[2]

The words "Let the man render unto his wife true friendship" give an interesting rendering in English of what must have been the French version of the Scriptures. I like that translation, also the concept it presents that God has every right to speak to a man about the matter of giving his wife her marriage-due.

A beneficial effect of a pastor making a conscious effort to make his wife happy is this: He will be contributing to the happiness of his children. A happy wife makes a happy mother, and a happy mother helps to make happy children.

17

Husband-Wife Relationships

Someone has said that while marriages are made in heaven they must be lived on earth.

Living together in the intimacy of marriage reveals to the marriage partners—even to a minister and his wife—how human they are. I wouldn't be surprised to learn that some wives of pastors feel that their husbands are among the most difficult persons in the world to live with. Some pastors may feel the same way about their wives.

People in the church and those with whom ministers have contact in the community treat him with courtesy and look up to him as a person with special qualifications for a role that has through the years given to ministers respect and affection. But a minister may be belittled in his own home. Why? Because his wife sees his failings and shortcomings as other people do not. She may hear others speak highly of his ability to help people to solve their interpersonal relationships but feel that he fails in such relationships at home.

Perhaps I can help you to have a more charitable attitude toward your husband.

First, I would make reference to the strong possibility that your husband, since he has chosen a profession in which he is expected to be a leader, has a strong, aggressive personality. Wouldn't you rather have a husband with such characteristics instead of one who is weak and allows other people—including yourself—to walk all over him?

A man who is deeply committed to the work to which the Lord has called him will want to give it his best, and other responsibilities will come second, third, fourth, and so on in his list of priorities. He will not want even his homelife to interfere with his work. Of course, he will need to learn to balance his roles of husband, father, pastor, citizen and neighbor.

Women often fail to understand that a man gets his feeling of achievement and fulfillment through his work. "A man . . . feels his work to be an extension of his personality; his job, his future, the relationships at work, usually are uppermost in his mind."[1]

"One of the basic emotional differences between the sexes is that men are basically 'do-ers,' while women are 'be-ers.' "[2] Understanding this distinction between a man and a woman can help you to accept the fact that your husband's interest in the home will not be as great as yours.

However, a man does not find total fulfillment in his work, just as most women do not find total fulfillment in homemaking. Each of you has needs other than your primary needs, and if you recognize these other needs your attitude will contribute to the happiness of your marriage union.

A wife may feel, for instance, the need of expressing her gift for writing or her musical talent. That man is wise who will recognize such a need. I remember talking with a young man at a Christian school who sought my counsel after I had talked to the men students at their chapel period on the subject of what a man going into Christian work should look for in the girl he considers asking to share his life. This young man told me he was fond of a young woman who had marked musical talents. Then he added, "But I am mediocre in the field of music. Do you think we could be happy together?"

I replied, "That would depend on your attitude. If you're afraid that she will outshine you, then I would advise that you not marry her. If you really love her as a person, you will want her to develop her gifts and to use them in the Lord's service."

Of course, I realize that many ministers' wives with musical abilities—to play the organ or piano, to sing, or direct a choir—are content not to perform often because they have chosen to remain in the background in order to avoid the appearance of being in competition with those in the church who have similar talents. A minister's wife needs to recognize that pastors and their wives come and go, but the people of the church stay; therefore, anything she and her husband can do to foster the development of their people and their talents through using their talents and abilities is for the good of the church.

However, in the relationship of a husband and wife, I think it's great if a husband rejoices in his wife's talents and capabilities. When I was about to enter into my second marriage, I was asked by friends, "How do you think your being known as a radio personality will affect your marriage?" My reply was something like this: "Mr. Nordland has enough 'on the ball' so that he doesn't need to keep his wife in the background. A man who is sure of himself and his own capabilities doesn't fear letting his wife develop and use her talents." After more than five years of marriage, I can say that he has been just wonderful in his attitude, and rejoices in the opportunities that are mine to minister to women through my radio programs, correspondence with listeners, and speaking engagements.

His attitude reminds me of something I read about love delighting in the loveliness of the beloved. The gifts of a woman and the gifts of a man (gifts of God) represent part of the personality of the person and, as such, should be a source of delight and not of envy. Such a view will eliminate all competitiveness in a marriage.

I really believe the best marriages constitute a mutual-admiration society. In such a marriage, husband and wife see things that call forth admiration, and they speak of them. That is a way of expressing love. Of course, we also express love when we try to help our marriage partner become a better person and effectively fulfill his role.

Sometimes I meet a wife who feels inferior to her husband because of a "culture gap" between them. Perhaps they married before he had finished his education, and she worked to help put him through school. This husband should not let his wife feel inferior to him. If college courses are available in her community and she wants to take them, he should encourage her to do this. If she isn't so inclined, he can let her know how he appreciates her as a woman, as his wife and mother of his children. I have heard ministers say, "I didn't marry my wife because she was a brain but for other qualities which I value."

A wife may have greater verbal skills than her husband, and a sense of correct grammar that is sharper than her husband's. Many men go through college and seminary and still use the English language in an awkward manner. (Often his speech reflects a pattern learned in his parental home.) I should think a man would value his wife's suggestions or her calling his attention to any mistakes in grammar or pronunciation. Sometimes a man doesn't know he is consistently mispronouncing a certain word, and doesn't look it up because he assumes his pronunciation is correct, having always said it that way. I know of a woman who told her husband, with much reluctance, that she had noticed he pronounced *mammoth* as *man*moth. He replied, "Dear, you are doing me a disservice if you don't call something like that to my attention." You see, he wanted to do his best in the pulpit, and she wanted that for him too.

One writer who addressed ministers about husband-wife relationships suggested that one way of keeping communication channels open between a minister and his wife was for the wife to evaluate her husband's sermon. I wondered when I read that whether evaluating a sermon on a regular basis would not make the minister more self-conscious about his preaching and cause him to wonder, "Will this come under her criticism?"

I also wondered if her criticizing his sermons would raise barriers to communication instead of keeping communication channels open. It seems to me that one of the most elemental rules of psychology to keep in mind in interpersonal relationships is this: Criticism nearly always raises a barrier. It would all depend on whether the husband asks the wife to do this on a regular basis. It has been a long time since I read the life story of that prince of British preachers, Charles Haddon Spurgeon, but if my memory serves me correctly, I read a reference to how Mrs. Spurgeon, on the day after her husband preached, would point out any mistakes in his grammar. According to the record, he welcomed such criticism.

Another barrier to communication may be this: a man's desire to use his home as a place where he escapes from the necessity to listen to people's troubles. For thirteen years I lived next door to a doctor and his family. His wife told me that since her husband listened to people reciting their symptoms and telling him of their aches and pains during his office hours, he didn't want to listen to her minor complaints when he was at home. Such an attitude can also be adopted by a pastor. Since he is constantly giving his attention and energy to various individuals, he thinks of his home as a place to be quiet and relax. And he doesn't want to listen to recitals of what went wrong at home during the day. This may be good for him but it may not be at all good for his wife.

In his desire to separate his work from his homelife, a man may make it a point not to discuss his work at home. It certainly is not wise for a man to discuss all the details of his work with his wife; but if he fails to say anything about his work, she may infer that he thinks she is unable to comprehend his problems and ideas. Or she may assume that he thinks she wouldn't be able to contribute a helpful response. And her sense of worth would be reduced. In my opinion, part of a man's ministry to his wife is making her feel significant as a person.

Another barrier to communication could be a minister's tendency to be critical of his wife because in his counseling of others he looks at them objectively and sees their faults. In such sessions it is not his business to look at faults in himself. However, I cannot refrain from pointing out that Dr. Paul Tournier, eminent Swiss psychiatrist, mentioned in one of his books that he found he was most helpful in counseling others when he revealed to his patients something of his own weaknesses, his own struggles. Since the pastor's wife has no pastor besides her husband, it may be difficult for her to have confidence in his counsel because he has at times been critical of her. However, if when he counsels her he is willing to disclose some of his struggles against his weaknesses, this could prove to be most helpful in breaking down any resentment she may feel.

It's difficult for a wife to observe her husband's patience with others and then fail to see the same patience exercised in his dealing with her and their children. A pastor who spends an hour patiently listening to someone's problem may become very curt with his wife when she presents to him problems that to him seem petty. But when she does this, it may be her way of saying, "Look here, I need attention too. I don't want to make all the decisions concerning our children."

A wife may at times fear that the women her husband counsels may transfer their affection to him, or that he might be attracted to one of them. Such fears may be implanted by someone's sly insinuation. Carolyn Blackwood, in her book *The Pastor's Wife,* referred to the reply one pastor's wife would make to any such insinuations:

She would chuckle and say, "Anyone else who can get him can have him!"[3]

Evidently this woman was confident of the power of the warmth of her love in his life, and she trusted her husband. However, some women who have "trusted" a husband have been keenly disappointed. I recall the comment of a woman who knew a minister (not as minister of the church their family attended but as a friend) who was guilty of unfaithfulness to his wife. This friend, who said their family had a very high regard for this minister and reported that he had been a strong spiritual leader in their community, commented, "His unfaithfulness started as a result of counseling *alone* those persons who should have been counseled only with another lady present. We definitely feel that it is very important for the pastor and his wife to counsel as a team those who ask for counsel who are of the opposite sex."

Of course, such safeguards may be necessary to protect a minister from the "wagging tongues" of gossips, but I wonder how effective his counseling can be with his wife present. Some women just wouldn't "open up" in the presence of the minister's wife—perhaps because they could not be sure that she would keep confidential what she heard. A minister might safeguard his reputation by seeing women at the church only if his secretary or other members of the church staff are in the church office. An alternative would be to ask the woman to see him at his home, with the explanation that his wife would be home but would remain in another part of the house if her presence wasn't wanted.

At any rate, if a pastor senses that his wife fears situations where women will transfer their affections to him, he can take ample measures to reassure her. She, on her part, can be warm, loving and responsive in her relationships with her husband and thus make it very unlikely that he will respond to any designing woman's overtures.

A wife can pray for her husband in his various contacts

with his co-workers in the church and the persons he counsels. I remember an occasion when I knew that an attractive, vivacious woman in her early thirties was to meet with my husband in his church office. The church secretary was present in the church office, carrying on her duties, so I was not concerned about possible "gossip." But I prayed for my husband to be given wisdom in conducting the interview, and that it might produce real spiritual results. How delighted I was when he came home for lunch that day to learn that she had decided to give her life to the Lord once more. She had received Him as her Saviour when she was much younger, but then during her years of widowhood she had responded to the attentions of a man who was not a believer in Jesus Christ. After marriage, he had told her he had married her because she was "a cute chick" and he thought she would be a help to him in his business contacts. That morning she set her face to serve the Lord, to bring up her two sons for Him, and to try to win her husband for Him. My every memory of her is of a beautiful Christian woman whose attractiveness had an extra dimension because of the radiance that comes from "rejoicing in the Lord," even though her circumstances weren't ideal. I tell you about this to illustrate how a pastor's wife can be her husband's helper by means of prayer. She can be a "prayer helper" in the way that Christians of the first century helped the apostle Paul (2 Co 1:11).

A Christian husband and wife who pray for each other both in the presence and the absence of the rest of their family are making use of one of the best ways for maintaining communication. And yet many couples do not pray together. I was shocked at the lack of response when, on the spur of the moment, I asked a group of churchwomen to whom I was speaking at a retreat, "How many of you pray with your husband daily?" Not one woman raised her hand—not even the preacher's wife. Someone has said that when a husband and wife can pray together openly and honestly they will remain sensitive to each other's feelings and attitudes. Also, when a husband and wife pray together at the close of the day, it would seem to require that they forgive one another. For how can we ask God to forgive us if we are not willing to forgive each other? If one of you has displayed anger during the day, asking forgiveness of your marriage partner before prayer at bedtime will enable you to fulfill the injunction of Ephesians 4:26: "Let not the sun go down upon your wrath."

Reading some of the books your husband has read and discussing them with him can be a means of communication as you share with each other your reactions to what the author expressed in his book. On an eight-day Florida vacation in 1970, I read four books in addition to swimming in the ocean, sightseeing, and eating out. Two of them were books which my husband read that week. I always enjoy reading, but I think I enjoyed those books in a special way because of our exchange of thoughts about certain portions of them that especially appealed to us.

Communication between husband and wife is stimulated by their spending time with other pastors and wives for sharing of their hopes, their disappointments, and their problems. Fun with other couples who are interested in the same type of recreational activities is good for you both.

Not only should you and your husband participate in times of relaxation and fun and spiritual fellowship with others, but you ought to plan for brief periods when you will be alone and can give undivided attention to each other. For a wife to go out with her husband to dinner, looking her prettiest and eating by candlelight, is good nourishment for those romantic feelings that can so easily taper off under the pressures of family and church life. However, don't wait for such occasions to tell your husband you love him. Tell him every day that you love him, and show your love in all the ways you can. Make it your aim that your love shall be a glowing, growing thing. I am reminded of some words shared with my husband

and me by Dr. Ralph Keiper. He said Dr. Donald Grey Barnhouse had given them to him and his wife when they were married. Dr. Keiper repeated them to us as Dr. Barnhouse repeated them to him—in French. And then he gave the translation: "May your love be more today than it was yesterday; may it be less today than it will be tomorrow."

18

Help Your Husband
but Don't Manipulate Him

Never underestimate the power of a woman! That's the thought that came to me one day when I listened to comments made by a radio announcer just prior to a classical music program featuring music by Sir Edward Elgar. (His best-known work, I would judge, is the familiar "Pomp and Circumstance" march played for so many graduation processionals.) The announcer mentioned Sir Elgar's wife who, though she was not trained as a musician, helped her husband by giving him her reactions to his music.

On one occasion after he had composed a piece of music and she had listened to it, she was of the opinion that the ending wasn't right. The next morning when he got up (earlier than she) he found a note pinned over that portion of the manuscript. The note said, "Dear, this ending isn't as good as it should be. I'm sure you can write a better ending." And he did. Nothing more was said about it, he later related, but since she said nothing more he was sure the new ending was satisfactory.

Another illustration of the power of a woman is found in Mrs. Alexander Maclaren, whose husband was a Baptist preacher in England, though he was born in Scotland. In middle age he discovered that he was wasting hours each week in deciding what to preach on Sunday, so at his wife's suggestion he began expository studies from a book of the Bible. Many of these were later published, and it is said that Maclaren's sermons have been, perhaps, next to Spurgeon's, the most widely read sermons of their time. They are still greatly appreciated, and his published expository notes have helped thousands of preachers in their sermon preparation. See what can come out of a man's ministry because of a suggestion by his wife?

If the minister has an ax to grind, his wife ought to gather up enough courage to suggest to him ways of varying his sermons. In some situations a wife might encourage her husband to take a positive stand on an issue, but then when she sits in church with the congregation she may cringe. It's easier to be brave if she thinks less of what various individuals think of the sermon and more of what God thinks of it.

However, a minister's wife must beware of the danger of putting into her husband's mind any thoughts that may create bad relationships between him and members of the church. I am reminded of the minister's wife mentioned by Eugenia Price in her book, *A Woman's Choice*. This thoroughly capable, intelligent woman, put her somewhat weaker-minded husband in painful competition with the members of his church board. She felt (and rightly so) that these men were holding her husband back in his efforts to expand their church. There seemed to be much to back up this woman's thinking, but there is nothing in Scripture to back up her attitude. One of the ladies of the church overheard this minister's wife give him his send-off from the parsonage back porch on his way to a board meeting. She patted him on the shoulder briskly, and said, "Now, go get 'em, honey! Don't let anyone get the best of you!"[1]

She may have thought she was giving good, laudable wifely encouragement. But because of her attitude (she was obviously filled with resentment against the men with whom her husband had to work), she was creating chaos. In such a situation resentments can build up. Certainly this is far different from the harmony and peace which are produced by the

Holy Spirit who wants us who are God's children to work together with one heart and mind and purpose.

If a minister's wife is aware that she is a strong personality, she should be careful lest she try to manipulate her husband, to maneuver him, or to manage him. In this connection I can't help but think of the Old Testament home of Isaac and Rebekah, where the wife was the dominant personality. How much grief she caused by her maneuvering and manipulating! Instead, she should have trusted God to work out what He had already promised concerning Jacob, her favorite son. He was the second-born of her twin boys and, as such, would be expected to be subservient to the firstborn. However, years earlier when she was about to give birth, the Lord said to her, "Two nations are in thy womb . . . and the one people shall be stronger than the other people; and the elder shall serve the younger" (Gen 25:23).

It takes faith—confidence in God—to wait for the working out of His purposes. The book of Isaiah says that our God is a God who "worketh for him that waiteth for him," and that those "that wait upon the LORD shall renew their strength; they shall mount up on wings as eagles; they shall run, and not be weary; and they shall walk, and not faint." And as we walk, we can walk not only in faith but in the power of the Spirit and in love. As we do this, we will be restrained from doing and saying those things that will cause discord in our church.

Another good reason for the wife's not manipulating, maneuvering, or managing her husband is this: he must feel total responsibility for his work. An aggressive or dominant wife can diminish her husband's feeling of accomplishment. Your most important help can be given to his physical and emotional interior, by undergirding your husband with love and understanding.

I have a friend whose husband, an ordained man, held a position of large responsibility in a Christian organization which required him to travel a great deal, both in this country and abroad. She seldom accompanied him on his trips while their sons were still at home because she preferred to stay home with them. One time I heard her respond to a question about her responsibilities by saying, "I preside over the ministry of the interior."

"The ministry of the interior" can be viewed in two ways: (1) as a ministry to your husband's physical needs by furnishing attractive, nourishing, well-balanced meals; (2) as a ministry to his emotional needs.

Since you, as a minister's wife, are the "minister of the interior" in the sense of planning menus, cooking and serving food, you should be aware that a man may eat plenty and not be well nourished. You will be helped in serving nourishing, well-balanced meals if you learn the principles of good nutrition. You can find books on the subject in the public library, and many cookbooks include a section on the subject. Not long ago I purchased the *Better Homes and Gardens New Cook Book* to replace the *Better Homes and Gardens Cook Book* which I had literally worn out and was reluctant to discard because I had inserted in this loose-leaf notebook so many recipes from friends which had become family favorites through repeated use over the years. I found in the new book a section of meal planning and nutrition which gives in brief compass information about the basic four food groups— milk, meat, vegetable-fruit, and bread-cereal. Also, inexpensive publications on the subject may be obtained from the Superintendent of Documents, U. S. Government Printing Office, Washington, D. C. 20402. You might want to send for a list of their publications.

At any rate, if you serve plenty of protein foods, fruits and vegetables and, as far as your husband is concerned, cut down on foods containing large amounts of carbohydrates (starches and sugars) and saturated fats, you won't be contributing to a problem that confronts many men today—overweight.

Overweight is one of the risk factors involved in heart disease, according to heart specialists. And heart disease is America's No. 1 killer.

Don't wait until your husband is overweight before you plan your menus carefully. I often say to young wives, "Begin this way of eating while you're young. It will be good for *you* as well as for your husband."

Please notice that I referred to a *way* of eating. I remember an occasion when I talked with an attractive woman in her thirties who had been following the Weight Watchers plan. During conversation I mentioned the "Weight Watchers diet," and she immediately interjected, "It's not a *diet;* it's a *plan* for eating." She was thoroughly enthusiastic about the plan, for she had lost seventy-six pounds in nine months.

When planning menus, in addition to restricting foods which are high in saturated fats (beef, pork, cream and butter), limit the number of eggs served. Why do I advise this? Because egg yolks are high in cholesterol. I am sure you will want to serve the kind of meals that will tend to keep the amount of cholesterol in your husband's blood vessels at a low level. A high cholesterol count, according to many doctors, is another risk factor related to heart and artery diseases. Young men in their thirties as well as men in their fifties and sixties die of heart attacks.

The heart specialist who cared for my husband in a Pennsylvania hospital after his heart attack in 1967 recommended that both my husband and I read a book entitled *Your Heart Has Nine Lives* by Alton Blakeslee and Jeremiah Stamler, M.D.[2] The hospital gift shop regularly carried paperback copies of this book in stock, so I procured one. I also bought a copy to give to my husband's daughter and her husband, with whom I stayed when I flew from Chicago to be with my husband during that period of hospitalization. As we read this book we were strongly impressed with the importance of young men (and their wives) learning how to forestall heart attacks by becoming aware of what to eat and what to avoid eating, by learning the value of exercise and the need for reducing tensions.

From what I have read about heart disease, tension is another factor which affects a person's cholesterol level. I have a friend who has been under the care of a famous heart specialist for more than fifteen years. My friend is very careful about adhering to his dietary restrictions. It was interesting to hear him say that he and his doctor discovered that when he was at home and working at the office his cholesterol level was higher than when he was away on vacation, even though he consistently followed the same dietary regime.

My friend's experience illustrates the benefit to be derived from an annual vacation. Some years ago I heard a doctor friend say to a young business executive who thought he was too busy to take a vacation, "You will do better work during the eleven months if you take a month's vacation."

Many ministers take a day off each week (or two half days). You may have to *insist* that your husband do this if you notice that he angers too quickly, laughs nervously, or cannot control his emotions when he's preaching. These are signs that he's in danger of an emotional explosion. And if a night's sleep doesn't give him enough strength for the next day, this means he's getting exhausted.

The best form of relaxation is exercise—tennis, golf, swimming, water skiing (or snow skiing), walking. Walking is ideal because it is something that can be done every day.

What about hobbies as forms of relaxation? It all depends on the man. Some men, instead of riding their hobbies, are driven by their hobbies. If a hobby isn't a take-it-or-leave-it proposition, it isn't a hobby. Someone has said that you should be able to let a hobby mold, rust or evaporate.

Even though golf may be considered physical exercise, it may create tension in men who take it too seriously. Dr. Henry Ostrom used to say, "You can master golf, or let it master you." If your husband plays golf so competitively that he becomes angry when he doesn't make a better score than those with whom he is playing, it would be wise for him to turn to some other form of recreation.

Many women begrudge a husband the time he spends with "the boys" playing golf, bowling, or fishing and hunting. A minister's wife will spare herself some emotional tension if she understands that most ministers, like most other men, enjoy times of recreation with other men.

But awareness of the enjoyment men derive from the companionship of other males should not deter you from letting your husband know of your desire for both of you to have fun, enjoy leisure, and relax together. However, *you* may be ready for fun and relaxation and your husband may not be. He may say, "I'm too busy."

When the schedule is the heaviest is when he needs diversion most, for living under constant tension takes too great a toll. You are seeking your husband's welfare when you persuade your husband that a change of pace is important. Don't ever let him feel guilty when he's relaxing. Dismiss from your mind the attitude some members of your congregation may have that the only day the minister really works is Sunday. He needs some time for relaxation each day and a complete day off each week. Both of you will need to *plan* times of recreation or you'll never get them.

I would also suggest that you keep your own schedule free so that you can accompany your husband on his day off. Of course, he may want to play golf with his favorite foursome. If he does, don't object. That will take only four hours or so, and you can spend the rest of the day together. Of course, if *you* learn to play golf, he may ask you to be his partner on those days when he can't get together with his male friends. Or your foursome could be made up of you and your husband and another couple.

Here's a good thought about the need for relaxation which I found in my reading: Just as the heart muscle rests between beats, the mind of man must idle along between periods of stress.

Jesus demonstrated that He recognized the need of a change of pace for His disciples when He said to them, after a strenuous preaching tour, "Come aside from the crowds, and rest a while."

The second aspect of your "ministry of the interior" is related to meeting your husband's emotional needs.

Since his life is one in which many demands are made upon him, I would suggest that you aim to make few demands upon him and to make your home the kind of place that your man will love to come home to.

Be responsive to your husband's demonstrations of love. Don't withhold yourself from him in order to punish him when you are upset about something he has done or hasn't done. There's scriptural basis for this advice in 1 Corinthians 7:5: "Defraud ye not one the other, except it be with consent for a time, that ye may give yourselves to fasting and prayer; and come together again, that Satan tempt you not for your incontinency."

If you meet your husband's emotional needs by a warm response to his demonstrations of affection, by your loving consideration of him in every aspect of homelife, by your sympathetic understanding, you will be meeting his needs in such a way as to make it difficult for him to be unfaithful to you. It's sad but true that every now and then a man becomes involved in an affair which ruins his reputation, takes him out of the ministry, and brings suffering and heartache to his wife and family and the church.

I was much impressed with the value of the characteristics of warmth and responsiveness in a woman after reading an article by Ardis Whitman titled "What Makes a Woman Unforgettable?" In answering this question Miss Whitman said,

"Beauty, certainly, does not harm, but some of the most intriguing women of our own generation have not been beautiful; . . . Perhaps the most universal answer is that the unforgettable woman is warm, responsive. In my own informal poll, more men voted for these qualities than for any other trait."[3]

I share with you excerpts from this article:

> You know that she is aware of you, . . . as a person in your own right. Her mind is hospitable to your ideas; her heart to your joys and sorrows. . . . She *cares*. . . .
>
> She expects to get and give a great deal in the run of an ordinary day. . . . Almost all greatly loved women have had this quality of joy in the moment. Look at the unforgettable women of history. How alive they were! What warmth and new discovery they brought to the people who knew them!
>
> She is a person in her own right. . . . She has a sense of personal security; . . . some of her joys are inward; . . . she has a satisfying existence in her own mind and imagination; . . . she need not always be entertained. She is not panicky about solitude and, since she wants privacy herself, she is willing to concede it to others. She has self-respect and a quality of serenity.
>
> . . . the unforgettable woman does not tiresomely insist on being understood. . . .
>
> "She is the kind of person who loves to love others," said one psychiatrist, . . .
>
> . . . a woman is unforgettable because she is good. . . . honorable, loving, courageous, and generous. . . .
>
> And she's brave. The real reason why more people are not warm and alive in their responses is that they refuse to take their share of being hurt. They'd rather pussyfoot around the edges of life than leap into it and take what comes. . . .
>
> . . . the unforgettable woman makes other people feel larger than life. She has the superlative gift of persuading people that they are more than they thought they were.[4]

The last-named gift produces the feeling in a person that was expressed by the teenage son of a friend in this way, "Mom, you made me feel ten feet tall!"

As I read Ardis Whitman's article I found a warm response in my thinking to the comment a much-traveled New York jeweler of foreign birth made as he glanced lovingly at his wife, busy in another room. "The woman a man never forgets is the one who gladly does the little things for his comfort, the little things which cost her time and effort. Do you know that when I come home at night my wife is always watching for me at the window of the kitchen? The garage is on the basement level and she runs downstairs and opens the door for me. Every night she welcomes me that way. How could a man forget a woman like that?"[5]

I hope my quotations from this article will give you insight into what I mean when I refer to a woman's filling her man's emotional needs in the husband-wife relationship. As a woman (a feminine personality) you complement the man, and you can make him feel manly. A womanly woman delights in her femininity and she delights in her husband's manly qualities. She is not in competition with him.

Another quality I want to emphasize is genuineness. This involves being yourself. Don't try to be anyone else. That God would use my personality was quite a revelation to me some years ago when I read an article in which Norman Grubb emphasized, "God will use *your* personality."

It is a wonderfully free-ing experience to come to value yourself as a person because God values you as a person. Since He has made you, you should not downgrade His creation. Although you may be very conscious of flaws in your character and deficiencies in your behavior, yet you are a significant person in God's sight. And since He desires that you be a better person than you are, He has made it possible for you to become that better person through the spiritual resources He has made available to you. But you are still *you.* The vitality and power of God's life *in* you—and yielded to by you—will give to your personality all the beautiful qualities that are described as "the fruit of the Spirit" in Galatians 5:22-23 and will enable you to act in a loving way toward other persons, as described in 1 Corinthians 13.

The means for spiritual growth and maturing are (1) daily contact with God through reading, studying, memorizing, and meditating on His Word and (2) prayer. Prayer, of course, includes listening to God as well as talking to Him.

Another means of spiritual growth is learning from the experiences of life as you allow God to apply the principles of His Word to particular situations in your life.

The apostle Paul referred to his learning from life's experiences in Philippians 4:11. He said, "I have learned, in whatsoever state I am, therewith to be content." Those who read these words are apt to apply it only to the area of material needs. However, these words spoke to me about more than material needs during the period of grief that I suffered when my first husband was afflicted for two years and seven months with a malignancy which caused his death, and when I went through bereavement and the experiences of widowhood.

I was especially helped by the Amplified Bible's rendition of these words: "I have learned in *any* and *all* circumstances, the secret of facing every situation" (v. 12). I was also helped by J. B. Phillips' paraphrase: "I have learned to be content, whatever the circumstances may be. I know now how to live when things are difficult and I know how to live when things are prosperous. In general and in particular I have learned the secret of facing either plenty or poverty" (Phil 4:11-12).

As I read this paraphrase, the words "in general and in particular" flashed new light on my experiences. I thought, *I had learned in general what the Bible had to say about the all-sufficiency of God's grace in any circumstance of life. But now I have learned in particular as the Spirit of God has applied God's Word to my particular circumstances.*

So I urge you to keep storing God's Word in your mind. Then, because the Holy Spirit will be able to retrieve from your "memory bank" what you have placed there through reading and studying the Bible, you will be fortified for times of special need that may occur in your life.

19

Loneliness

"A person can be lonely in a crowd" is a statement we often hear. This is the kind of loneliness a pastor's wife may feel, even though she has many acquaintances and friends.

Wallace Denton, in his book *The Role of the Minister's Wife,* says that the loneliness of ministers' wives "arises, not out of an absence of people, but out of their lack of deep, meaningful relationships with these people. Loneliness is dispelled when one whole person confronts another whole person in love. Many ministers' wives seem to have difficulty finding persons with whom they can be whole selves."[1]

He referred to one wife who pointed out that "loneliness can stem from the fact that no one shares experiences and convictions that the minister's wife perceives as significant."[2]

Who are the people whom she might consider significant? Persons who can be challenged, who are spiritually adventurous.

Another factor contributing to the loneliness of a minister's wife is the tendency of people to look on her as being different—due, no doubt, to her symbolic role. To illustrate, perhaps you have heard a minister describe how he became engaged in a lively, animated conversation with someone at the barbershop or on an airplane. But when he was asked, "What do you do?" and replied, "I'm a minister of the gospel," the flow of conversation was no longer as free as it had been. Something similar can happen to a minister's wife at a club meeting or PTA meeting.

Perhaps you are thinking, *Well, ministers' wives have close friendships with other ministers' wives.* Few ministers' wives, according to one survey, have close relationships with other ministers' wives. One reason is busyness. Another could be doctrinal differences. Still another could be the competitiveness that exists between the respective churches their husbands pastor.

My husband says he never likes to think of one church being in competition with another, for there is so great a spiritual need in the world and so many persons who don't know Jesus Christ as Saviour that there is room for all to work. When Jesus was on earth He said, thinking of all the people who needed the message He was sending His disciples to proclaim, "The fields are white already unto harvest." I like the way the Living New Testament paraphrases what He said: "Vast fields of human souls are ripening all around us, and are ready now for reaping. The reapers will be paid good wages and will be gathering eternal souls into the granaries of heaven! What joys await the sower and the reaper, both together!" (Jn 4:35b-36).

On another occasion Jesus said, "The harvest truly is plenteous, but the labourers are few; pray ye therefore the Lord of the harvest, that he will send forth labourers into his harvest" (Mt 9:37-39).

There is plenty of work for all who serve the Lord in the ministry of local churches; therefore, there should be no spirit of competitiveness between churches and their pastors. I have found, through the experience of living in both small towns and large cities as a pastor's wife, that the spirit of competitiveness between churches is greater in small towns. At least I was more conscious of it there than when I lived in a metropolitan area.

Another reason why a pastor's wife may not have close relationships with other ministers' wives is this: She and her husband are very close companions, both in the work of the church and in their recreational activities.

One wife coped with her loneliness and lack of close friends by carrying on an extensive correspondence with old friends. She said, "I would advise any young minister's wife to learn the art of letter writing and to learn to treasure old friends." Denton, commenting on this advice, said, "A friendship by mail is better than none at all, but it would take a legion of letters to be as meaningful as one 'live' friend."[3]

Denton also observed that "the loneliness of ministers' wives arises not out of their lack of friends alone. They have a church full of friends. But it arises out of the problem of relating very closely and personally with a few individuals in the church simply as Mary Smith, not as 'the minister's wife.' As the wife of the minister, she is cast into a leadership role. An understanding of the psychology of leadership indicates that this immediately establishes certain barriers and tends to set her apart as being different. Loneliness is the natural sequence of this isolation, this 'differentness.' The ever-present problem of the leader is to maintain a balance between distance from his followers without moving to the other extreme of familiarity. The effective leader can probably never develop intimate relationships with those whom he leads without jeopardizing his role as a leader. In this sense, the minister's wife confronts a dilemma. She must either learn to live with her loneliness, seek other outlets, or be willing to run the risks involved in closer relationships within the congregations. Probably each wife must decide for herself what ways are most meaningful to her in coping with this loneliness."[4]

20

Women of the Church
and the Pastor's Wife

I was so glad when a schoolteacher who attends the same church as my husband and I do told me that a woman who had listened to my radio talks on the pastor's wife had said, "Well, the problems of a minister's wife aren't much different from the problems of other women," and since she had been helped by listening, she told a friend who wasn't a listener about the program, and she too began listening.

This came as encouragement to me when I had come to the point where I was saying to myself, "Frances, this series is getting a bit long."

Not long after that the wife of a young minister told me, after a friend had called her to tell her about this series and she had listened to several, "I liked your approach of presenting this information to churchwomen as well as to wives of pastors."

I do hope that an increased understanding of the problems a pastor's wife faces may cause you to be more sympathetic and thus more kind and considerate, and to pray for her. And to show friendship.

You may say, "But she has so many friends." True. But if she is like most ministers' wives I know, she doesn't have intimate friends within the congregation. And many a pastor's wife doesn't have her family nearby. I think that not having intimate friends or family nearby is felt more by the woman whose husband pastors a church in a small town or a rural

area. I will never forget a statement made by Dr. Vernon Mc-
Gee: "Small towns can be very cruel."

I enjoy very much the letters I receive from a woman who
is the wife of an Illinois farmer and who with her family attends a rural church. This woman shares with me, among
other things, her feelings concerning her pastor's wife. In one
letter she said:

> It is a great joy to see how God is working in the life of
> our pastor's wife, for whom I've prayed so much. About this
> time every year [her letter was toward the close of the winter,
> a time when some people become despondent because of the
> effect of a succession of gray, cloudy, damp days] she has
> become quite despondent and discouraged, and this has
> troubled me. However, this year she continued to remain in
> good spirits and isn't thinking of herself so much. For some
> time now I've been going to see her about once a week. We
> talk about the things of God and pray for others. I had want-
> ed to help her, and it came to me to do this, for I felt God
> has wanted me to encourage her all I can. She's a wonder-
> ful woman, and has been greatly used of God, in my opinion.
>
> The first time I heard your broadcast you were speaking
> about pastors' wives, but our radio was giving us trouble at
> that time, and I didn't hear all you said. I hope you'll talk
> again on how we can help these women, and how we should
> consider them. I wonder how many church people realize
> that when the preacher is harshly and unfairly criticized his
> wife is hurt too?
>
> Not long after I was saved, our pastor went through a
> time of great discouragement, and he seemed so lonely. His
> wife also was suffering, and I had such a great burden for
> them that I cried out to God for them. I have felt God
> wanted me to do all I can for them. Others in our parish are
> burdened also.

When I answered this woman's letter, I told her about a
book by Dorothy Pentecost entitled *The Pastor's Wife and the
Church*.[1]

Several months later my correspondent wrote to me saying,

Thank you very much for recommending the book *The Pastor's Wife and the Church.* I bought two copies and left one at the parsonage on a day when our pastor's wife had been particularly busy—"on the go." She seemed quite thrilled with the gift. Since then we have discussed some parts of the book at various times. I wish you knew this little woman. She is just precious, and has done much for many by her teaching and the example of her life.

Not long after I was saved, I felt God wanted me to do all I could for her and her husband. They've had a hard time of it here. There have been many heartaches, and when I've been aware of this I've hardly been able to stand it.

Several months ago, as I was having my devotions, I felt led to read in Luke 7. I read about John the Baptist (then in prison) sending his disciples to question Jesus. Jesus sent back a message to encourage John and spoke to those who were present about John. After reading that, it seemed I was told to go and encourage and comfort God's servant, our pastor's wife, who is doing much work for God. I told her, among other things, that she is being prepared for more work some day. It came to me also that I must be very careful with her, and treat her with all consideration, kindness, patience, respect, and compassion, and that she is dearer to God than I can know. . . . I had not been a Christian long, and it seemed rather strange to get a message like this. I haven't told it to anyone.

As I was having devotions recently, and wondering what I could do for her as a servant of the Lord, it came to me that I should continue to love her and pray for her. That is no small thing. At times she doesn't have much confidence in herself, and occasionally is depressed. She's a very brilliant woman, a highly gifted teacher, and devoted to the Lord. She's a wonderful woman; Jesus in her heart makes her wonderful. She had much to do with my becoming a Christian, so she means much to me.

And she closed her letter by telling me that she didn't come to know Christ as her Saviour until after she came to the Midwest from a distant state. She said, "I'm very thankful to God for His providence and love in bringing me here to be instructed by this pastor and his wife and also to where I could listen to you."

In still another letter, a couple of months later, she wrote,

> How grateful I am to God for the teachers, ministers, and Christian friends He gives us! It's one of the most wonderful ways He blesses us.
>
> Thank you very much for the material you enclosed on grumbling about the preacher. I'm passing it around for others to read. I've prayed so much for our church and congregation, and sometimes I get very discouraged, but I continue to pray.
>
> Our pastor and his family are now on vacation. In answer to our prayers they have gone to visit the wife's parents. I've felt sorry for her living so far away from them. She did admit once that she was a little homesick. The last time they visited her parents was three years ago. This time her family sent money for their traveling expenses. They have had much expense lately for medical treatments for their little girl. . . . With all the problems they have, it's wonderful to see how God is taking care of them.
>
> Before she left, the pastor's wife and I had a talk, and she told me of some wonderful answers to prayer in her life. I rejoiced with her, for she has had some great personal difficulties. She has said that though her husband's salary isn't large they feel very rich when they see how God is using them and working in the lives of people in the congregation. She says she has visited in wealthy churches with fancy parsonages where there seemed to be little in the way of *spiritual* riches.

In my opinion, this woman of sensitivity of the right kind, sensitivity to the inner needs of her friends, must have been a great source of encouragement to her pastor's wife.

Eugenia Price in her book *Make Love Your Aim* talked

about *who* needs love. She referred to the unquestioned need of children for love, to the need of parents for love from their children, to the need of employers for love, of friends for love from friends, of the bereaved for love. And she included clergymen as needing love.

> Clergymen need love. They are expected to give it day in and day out, night in and night out to the members of their churches, whether they feel like it or not. But few parishioners love their pastor enough not to be insulted if he is just too weary or too busy to visit them in person and sends his assistant instead. [2]

I would add, "The *wives* of clergymen also need love from the church people." That's why I shared with you excerpts from letters written by a woman who opened up her heart to me to reveal a caring love for her pastor's wife.

"Go thou, and do likewise."

21

Can You Keep a Secret?

If anyone were to ask you who can best keep a secret—men or women—I'm quite sure that you would answer "Men." Yes, even women feel that way.

In my files I found a clipping titled "Keeping Secrets" which goes like this:

> It's no secret to either sex that women seem to have a good deal of trouble keeping confidences. For one thing, they talk more in general. [Oh, oh, I can almost hear your objections!] Then too, their emotions influence them more than thought or logic. That's why they're so apt to burst out with news and think later. Avoid confidences especially with women friends under twenty or over forty. These are the ages when they're most likely to betray confidences; when they're younger to back up boasts, when they're older to be important and "in the know." But ironically it's either a feast or a famine on the feminine verbal front. When women have been famous spies, they've been top-notch, and notoriously close-mouthed.

So, you can't generalize about women being more talkative than men, and unable to keep confidences.

It's too bad when church members feel that a pastor or his wife cannot be trusted to keep confidential what they know about persons who have gone to him for counseling.

One woman at a session for pastors' wives which was part of a Bible conference schedule submitted this question to be answered during the question-and-answer period: "I hear pastors say, 'I never confide any of my ministry to my wife.' Is this proper?"

I read in a book of advice for pastors' wives that there is a strong consensus of opinion among experienced clergymen that confidences placed in the hands of the minister are his alone. While this is sound reasoning, the procedure is emotionally untenable for some wives.

"I don't know anything about anything" ought to be a happy theme song instead of a complaint. In the area of personal matters confided to a pastor, ignorance can be bliss for the wife.

Of course, a wife may argue during the half-glow, half-tension phase of early marriage that a sound marriage is based on mutual sharing, with nothing held back. And the bridegroom may respond to the appealing plea to some extent. It's a romantic but impractical basis for sharing other people's confidences. A man new in the ministry is more apt to succumb to his wife's wishes, for he has so little to share and is probably eager to talk it over with someone anyway.

Don't pump your husband for information. However, if he shares with you information which ought to go no further, be sure you tell no one. Once you reveal a confidence, it is easily repeated; if you don't reveal a confidence, it cannot be repeated. No one can misquote silence.

There may be times when a minister wants to verbalize the problem, but he doesn't need to let his wife know the identity of the person. He may want her to pray about the problem, but she doesn't need to know the identity of the individual concerned, for God knows without her mentioning the individual's name.

Once word gets around that a minister or his wife can't keep confidences, their ministry is crippled. He is viewed as an untrustworthy person, and she is too. A slip of the tongue on the part of the minister or his wife can haunt them wherever they go. Someone always knows someone, or has an Aunt Susan, in the next parish. Our past pursues us to the grave.

When we lived in Michigan, word came to us from California about what an evangelist who had conducted a series of meetings in our town had said in a California church about our church and its pastor. Little did the evangelist know that in the audience was a woman who had lived in our town and knew the church and pastor well. At the close of the meeting she went to the evangelist and confronted him with what he had said and plainly told him that she knew he was completely mistaken.

It would be well if every minister and minister's wife—yes, every Christian—would examine their conversation by these three questions: Is it true? Is it kind? Is it necessary to repeat this?

I like this bit of verse about

WHAT YOU SAY
What you say in a hurry
May cause you much worry.
So weigh your words well—
What you'd say.
Ill-chosen expressions
Oft give wrong impressions.
So think first, then speak.
It will pay.

WILLIAM LANGHORST

You may be able to discipline yourself so that you would die before you would repeat a word of a confidence. But how much of what you know will be revealed in your voice, your facial expression, your eyes? Perhaps you will feel moral revulsion at what you know. Can you be sure your revulsion won't show? If you don't know the problems that have been confided to your husband, you won't have to worry about your feelings showing. If you get your information from other sources than your husband, you'll be able to act naturally and reveal all the love you feel.

Sometimes a wife must know a confidence, for there are situations where she can be a help. You may need to know that certain persons are under stress—without being informed about the specific problem—in order to use care in approaching these individuals about cooperating in certain church projects.

It's agonizing for any woman to be so near and yet so far from such interesting information because women like to know the details of the lives of other persons. I wonder whether we should call this female curiosity or loving interest?

If you have an excessive amount of curiosity about the lives of others, it may be that your own life needs some attention. I'll share with you an answer given by a psychologist to a woman who confided this problem to him: "I always find myself giving out unasked-for information. It doesn't seem to matter whether I'm with a close friend or somebody I hardly know. In no time at all, I tell about private things I ought to keep quiet about. Afterward I feel awful and worry about it for days. But then I go and open my big mouth all over again. Why do I do this?"

The psychologist pointed out that her problem was a common symptom but that, like some other emotional problems, it could stem from one of a number of roots. The most common of these is a need to be liked. In effect, though not in words, the person is saying, "Look, I'm giving you something —secret information—so please like me."

Another root is curiosity about other persons' private affairs. It's as if the one who is divulging secrets is saying, "I'm giving you secret information, so please give me some too."

Such a failing also reveals a need to be entertaining and to be admired; a repressed (hidden) desire to express hostility and to hurt others through malicious gossip; a repressed de-

sire to hurt oneself, due to unconscious self-hatred; or a repressed desire to exhibit oneself.

What we talk about reveals a great deal about ourselves.
Jesus recognized this when He said, "Out of the abundance
of the heart the mouth speaketh" (Mt 12:34). The apostle
James, who devoted a sizable portion of his epistle to the power of the spoken word, said, "If any man offend not in word,
the same is a perfect man" (Ja 3:2).

There's nothing like a review of what we said during the
course of one day to convince us that we are not perfect.
Since you are not perfect, now and then you may feel the
need to pray somewhat like this:

> Dear Lord,
> I come confessing.
> There are times when I talk too much.
> There are times when I repeat things which I have no right
>   to repeat.
>> I pass on a story which may not be entirely true or add
>>   my own embroidered flourish to a tale in the telling.
> Father, forgive.
> This is a sin of commission—
>   and a dreadful betrayal of confidence.
> Forgive,
>   and help me remember to keep a deliberate and constant
>   check on my tongue.
> Keep safe within me the hurts and secrets that others
>   have shared,
>   for they are a trust.
>
> . . . .
>
> Keep safe within me those communications
>   which were entrusted to me for safekeeping.
>   Amen.[1]

Even though on the basis of 1 John 1:9 we know that
God is faithful and just to forgive us our sins when we confess them to Him, and to cleanse us from all unrighteousness,

we still need to "keep a deliberate and constant check" on our tongues. Once we have said the words which we ought not to have said, we cannot recall them.

It is said that the late Peter Marshall enjoyed telling the story of the naughty little boy who squeezed toothpaste in zebralike stripes across the back of a dozing cat, then shook all the apples off the trees in an orchard, and clipped chunks of hair from the head of a sleeping barber. In the movie cartoon from which Mr. Marshall got the story, the boy was required to go back and put everything right. In real life it isn't as easy to put things right as in fantasyland, for you can't push toothpaste back into the tube from which it has been squeezed. You can't expect to reattach apples to the tree from which they have been shaken and expect them to grow and ripen. And once hair has been cut, the results have to be lived with for a while.

Similarly, once we have betrayed a confidence, we cannot cancel what has been said. Your speech, as far as confidences are concerned, should be governed by this one-word rule: silence. Remember, silence can never be quoted or misquoted.

Make daily use of these prayers from the book of Psalms: "Set a watch, O LORD, before my mouth; keep the door of my lips" (141:3) and "Let the words of my mouth, and the meditation of my heart, be acceptable in thy sight, O LORD, my strength, and my redeemer" (19:14).

Or you could pray in a modern idiom: "Lord, nudge me lest I say too much."

22

Jealousy

One reason for the excessive desire of some women to know what goes on behind the minister's study door is this: jealousy. It isn't easy to know that other women are sharing their innermost secrets with your husband.

A minister's wife who wrote to me about her struggle to overcome jealousy said that she viewed her jealousy as a sin which was dragging her deeper into defeat every day. She said, "My husband is wonderful. As we have talked about this problem, he has prayed with me about it. In fact, he has prayed daily with me. I'm all right for a while, but the devil keeps after me. I want to stop all this confusion I'm bringing to my family."

Too often Christians blame the devil for emotional conditions that are the result, possibly, of some family situation in childhood. For instance, some persons, during childhood, were never sure of the love of their parents, and they grew up feeling they couldn't hold the love of anyone.

In the book *The Art of Understanding Your Mate* by Cecil G. Osborne, in a chapter titled "Conflicts that Mar Marriages," are these comments on the subject of jealousy or possessiveness: "Being abandoned and feeling rejected in childhood creates deep insecurities in a child. These can later manifest themselves in various neurotic behavior patterns. Extreme jealousy or possessiveness usually stems from some emotional deprivation in early childhood."[1]

These comments are illustrated by a letter from a radio listener:

> I suffered many years from the heartbreaking disease of jealousy. I don't think anyone suffers as much as the one afflicted with it. But life is miserable for all whose lives she touches. I was an only child from a broken home. My husband was faithful. I knew this, but it helped little. Because of my jealous attitude I would be hurt beyond words if any woman would sit on a couch next to my husband, even in my presence. In the days that followed, I would make life miserable for him. But *I* was the one who was suffering the most, and I hated myself for being so very foolish.
>
> After I accepted the Lord as my personal Saviour I took this problem to Him and left it with Him. I cannot say how or when my jealousy was taken away, but the Lord heard my cries for help, and I praise Him for answering my prayers. I am a new person.

This woman (not a pastor's wife) testified that she had been afflicted with jealousy for more than twenty-five years, and is now free. In her case her new relationship with the Lord cared for an area of her life in which she had previously experienced defeat. But what about the woman who is a Christian and is still troubled with jealousy? If her problem is extreme possessiveness and persistent feelings of jealousy, she may need the help of a counselor.

Of course, if she tells her husband about how she feels, this will bring the problem into the open, and as he prays for her in her presence and she prays in the presence of her husband, confessing her weakness in this area to the Lord and asking for His guidance and help, she will make progress in overcoming jealousy, I'm quite sure.

As a minister's wife you can expect you'll have a minor skirmish with jealousy now and then, and you will want to know what goes on when your husband counsels women. But your battle will be half won if you have the fundamental conviction that you must respect the sacred trust someone else puts in your husband.

Even if you could be trusted never to reveal confidences, think of the time involved for a busy pastor, when he is tired, to go over a case that contains much that is unpleasant. Control your curiosity and make it your aim to help him to unclutter his mind of such problems. Your time together is precious!

When a young woman marries a minister she would do well, ahead of time, to reconcile herself to the fact that many women will look to her husband for advice in times of sickness, sorrow and trouble. Anyone who has lived in the home of a physician knows that his wife must trust him when he is alone with women. The pastor is a physician of souls. Sometimes his ministry will be to the sort of women whom our Lord befriended, partly because no one else would treat them like human beings who needed salvation.

For the sake of protecting a minister's reputation in view of the kind of women with whom he may have to deal, and in view of the natural tendency for people to gossip, many a minister asks his wife to accompany him on some of his calls. However, most people who need counseling will open up more completely if a third party isn't present. If a minister senses that a woman who has asked for counsel would not want his wife to be present, he may arrange for that individual to come to his study at the church and then keep the door open between his study and the secretary's office. Or, if he has no secretary, he could invite the woman to come to the parsonage, letting her know that his wife will be in the house but not present for the interview.

I realize (and I say this with sadness in my heart) that occasionally a minister has proved unfaithful to his wife. When this happens, the story is played up in the press—to the hilt. But who writes up the stories of the thousands of ministers who are happily married, who are faithful to wife and children, unselfishly serving God and their parishioners?

If someone whispers in your ear, "Aren't you afraid to have your husband counseling all those women who come to him for advice?" you might feel hurt for two reasons: (1) because anyone would imply that your husband might philander, and (2) because anyone would think you didn't trust him.

Believe in your man. Tell yourself, "He loved me enough to choose me out of all the girls he knew to be his wife." Be confident that he considers his love for you to be a lifetime commitment to you. There will always be prettier women than you. And, as you grow older, there will always be younger, more attractive women.

However, even though you know that marital love is not to be based entirely on physical attractiveness, I would advise you to give careful thought to present an attractive exterior and a gracious, charming manner which issues from a beautiful "interior" (see 1 Pe 3:4). Do this *because* your husband loves you and *because* you love him. Trust your husband. Love him. Say so and show him so.

The sure way of getting victory over jealousy is to allow the Holy Spirit to control you and produce in you His fruit of love. God, speaking through the apostle Paul, has given us a wonderful description of love in 1 Corinthians 13. In J. B. Phillips' paraphrase of this chapter, he uses this phrase to describe love: "It is not possessive." This is in contrast to jealousy, which is overpossessive. Love is described not only as "not possessive" but as "not touchy," which is in contrast to the touchiness with characterizes jealous individuals. Another mark of jealousy is distrustfulness. However, love is described by Mr. Phillips in his paraphrase as knowing "no limit to its endurance, no end to its trust, no fading of its hope," with the ability to "outlast anything."

23

Gifts

The ministry of a man who starts filling the role of pastor in his middle twenties may add up to forty years or more. During those years he and his wife will be invited to perhaps hundreds of weddings. In addition, she will be invited to baby showers and bridal showers. A young minister and his wife, just starting out in their first pastorate, may wonder as they receive invitations to such events, *What will we do about gift-giving?* They may also wonder what they should do about birthdays, anniversaries, and graduations of church members. Should they give gifts just as everyone else does, or should they give just a token gift and give the same to all? Should they give only to church members and not to those who attend regularly? Should they give a gift only when they are formally invited? Should they give only to families who customarily give gifts to the pastor's family?

The pastor has a relationship with every family of the church. Therefore the number of gifts required and the expense, were he to give gifts in the same manner as one does with one's own family and close friends, put his gift-giving and that of his wife in a different light than the gift-giving of most families.

The first wedding in the first parish marks the time when the pastor and his wife must come to a decision about gifts to couples at whose wedding he officiates. Whatever the decision, one cardinal rule should be followed: Be absolutely consistent! He can be consistent by giving the same devotional book or a Bible to each couple in whose marriage ceremony he participates.

When we were first married and my husband and I couldn't quite decide what we should do about giving gifts to those for whom my husband performed a marriage ceremony, I sought advice from an older minister's wife. She said, "When a minister performs a wedding ceremony *he* is giving to the couple." Actually, he usually gives of himself for two evenings—one evening for rehearsal and the next for the wedding ceremony. And if it is his practice to give marriage counseling prior to the marriage, he has given one or two evenings to this important ministry.

The safest policy is this: Refrain from giving gifts to members of your congregation. I realize that following this policy will not be easy for a generous, warmhearted pastor and wife who are so aware of how often they receive. But once you make an exception to your rule you may encounter some unhappy consequences. News about a pastor's gift to a parishioner travels rapidly. Most laymen just cannot resist mentioning that a particular gift is from the minister and his wife, and there will always be those among the parishioners who will remember what you gave to someone else and make comparisons.

When I was invited to baby showers and bridal showers I gave gifts at such affairs because I considered myself a friend of the bride or the expectant mother just as much as other women who were present. Of course, because I was the pastor's wife I was invited to all of such affairs for members of the church, while others might not be invited to that many showers. As a result, I had to purchase a few more shower gifts than did others in the congregation.

Christmas gift-giving to parishioners should be absolutely ruled out, in my opinion. But it seems that some ministers do give gifts to some of their parishioners, for in one book of ad-

vice to ministers I found this paragraph: "To give gifts is a
financial burden which will increase as the years go by. He
may in time feel frustration, even resentment, about Christmas
gift-giving when he has to start early in the year to prepare for
the Christmas deadline, because of the precious time and
energy stolen from his current parish and his family for these
personal obligations. A choice must be made as in every
other area of your life: what is going to have priority on your
time, attention and money?"

However, a minister ought to be alert to the danger to
one's soul to be always receiving and not giving. My husband
and I gave to the support of our church and its missionary
program just as we expected any faithful member of our
church to give. We decided to give at least a tenth of our
gross income. How could we conscientiously teach our people
systematic, proportionate giving if we ourselves were not
giving in that way? Yet I have known ministers who said they
felt that because they were ministers and serving God in that
way they were excused from systematically giving a portion
of their income. I do not judge them, for God is the Judge of
His servants. We read in Romans 14, "Each man stands or
falls to his own master."

Of course, most important of our gifts is the constant giving
of ourselves in loving service as a living sacrifice to the Lord
for the benefit and spiritual maturing of God's people as well
as for the purpose of bringing those who do not yet know the
Lord into a life-giving relationship with Him through faith in
Jesus Christ as Saviour.

Ministers and their wives need not only to learn the grace
of *giving* but also the grace of *receiving* gifts. I had never
thought much about this until (when I was about thirty years
old) a missionary nurse who was staying at our home said to
me, "Frances, I've had to learn the grace of receiving. When
I was employed as a nurse I had the joy of giving to God's

servants. Now that I am a missionary candidate I must learn the grace of receiving."

We read in the Bible this saying of Jesus: "It is more blessed to give than to receive" (Ac 20:35). Anyone who has practiced giving has discovered the blessings and happiness which come from giving. Not only is it more blessed to give than to receive but it is *easier* to give than to receive.

In the early years of my experience as a minister's wife, a period when ministers' salaries were low because our country was going through an economic depression, many people didn't have cash available and thus were unable to give financially to the support of the church and its pastor. But some of our parishioners who were farmers gave other gifts— chickens, eggs, potatoes. When the market price of potatoes was low I was given bushels and bushels of potatoes which were heaped in a big pile in the parsonage basement—that part of it which was a dirt floor instead of a concrete floor.

One dear Dutch lady washed and cut the stems off green beans (a whole bushel of them!) and then put them through a device which cut them into thin slices. These I processed in quart jars in a hot water bath, and they were a welcome addition to our meals during the winter months.

Farmers invited us to their farms to pick strawberries and raspberries—as many as we wanted. Another farmer was a grape-grower, and he gave us grapes. Some of these we enjoyed fresh, and some we processed for grape juice and grape jelly. Then, since we lived in the fruit-growing section of western Michigan, we enjoyed the abundance of pears, peaches and apples. I recall a rainy Labor Day which I spent in the basement of our parsonage canning apples that had to be processed almost immediately because they were windfalls. I canned seventy-eight quarts of applesauce that year. I have often thought since then, *It's too bad we didn't purchase a freezer until after we moved to the big city of Chicago!*

Well, I hope you haven't minded my reminiscing and sharing with you a bit of what life was like for me in our first two pastorates.

I would sum up my advice about accepting gifts in this way: Accept gifts with loving appreciation, even if you already have more than enough of what is given. Just as a gift without the giver is bare, a gift without a grateful recipient has failed in its purpose. If you mumble a subdued unenthusiastic thanks, you rob the giver of some of the joy of giving.

Most gifts come as an expression of gratitude for some special service rendered or to convey love and appreciation in an outward symbol. Some gifts may be given out of feelings of guilt and a desire to "make atonement" for behavior for which the giver is sorry. Sometimes it is easier for an individual to give a gift than to apologize.

There are those persons, too, who are generous to the minister and his wife with a view to dominating one or the other. My husband and I saw this motive in a woman in one of our churches. However, since we recognized her desire to exercise dominance in the church, we were alert and didn't allow ourselves to be drawn into too close an association with her. Our relations with her required tact to the nth degree.

Even though you sense subconscious motivations for some gift-giving, you can be quite sure that most gifts are a genuine expression of love and appreciation.

However, don't assume that people do not love and appreciate you if you fail to receive gifts as tangible expressions of their love and appreciation. Sometimes national or cultural backgrounds make a difference in how people express their love and gratitude. If most of the people are of a culture that counts hard work, thrift, and economizing to be admirable virtues, they may be reluctant to give special gifts to their pastor. I feel this was so in one of our pastorates, for after we had moved to another pastorate numerous members of that church asked one another, "Why didn't we do more for them while they were here?" For years after, when I had contact with persons in that church, I experienced hearing some of them relate how much they appreciated my husband's Bible-teaching ability and what his teaching had meant in their spiritual growth.

At any rate, gift-giving can be haphazard. You may receive a gift one year on your birthday or anniversary and not the next. The difference is usually this: the laymen who are in leadership positions.

Even though tangible expressions of appreciation do give a lift to your morale, you should be able to serve the Lord and the people of your church in the spirit expressed by the apostle Paul in Philippians 4. He was able to get along happily whether he had much or little. But when, after long delay, the Christians sent him a gift, he said, "What makes me happiest is the well-earned reward you will have because of your kindness" (Phil 4:17, Living NT).

24

Should a Pastor's Wife
Seek Outside Employment?

A few years ago I received a letter from a radio listener who said,

> Many of our church-member ladies listen to your "Woman to Woman" program every day and enjoy your comments and are blessed and encouraged. They have asked me to write to you and ask you to give your unbiased opinion about some church responsibilities to God.
>
> What is your opinion of a pastor's wife holding a secular job when there is no financial need? We are members of a very large church and have felt for many years that the Women's Society is a very important part of the church program. We have a real burden for the souls of unsaved women, and because of this many dedicated women sacrificially give of their time, talent, and money. As a result many women have come to know the Lord Jesus Christ as Saviour through the women's meetings and efforts.
>
> I have fond memories of the years when I accompanied our previous pastor's wife each week to visit the sick in their homes or in the hospitals, call on women, and attend meetings where she spoke, or provide the special music. We also worked in the church kitchen together.

While I think it is ideal for the pastor's wife not to accept employment outside her home, I have noticed in my contacts with pastors' wives that more and more of them are employed. Some of the reasons they have given for seeking employment are:

1. A present financial need because the husband's salary isn't sufficient to meet the expenses of a growing family. I can sympathize for I remember the years when my first husband's salary lagged far behind the inflation spiral and we had three growing boys to feed and clothe, besides heating a large parsonage and purchasing and operating a car, with no car allowance provided by the church. I decided to work and secured an attractive position in a school office. However, I only worked for a month or so because I became ill with an overactive thyroid. During the brief period when I was employed we felt the displeasure of some members of the congregation. Their attitude was hard to understand, but, as one church member put it, the board of the church must have assumed that the pastor and his family could live on less than they did.

2. A future financial need. This would involve concern about savings for the children's college education and for one's retirement years. In another church than the one mentioned, my concern about these two items caused me to seek employment since most of the women of the church were working and there were no daytime women's meetings. I felt I wasn't neglecting the work of the church, for I attended all meetings (including Wednesday night prayer meetings and the monthly women's meetings). I also conducted a girls' club meeting twice a month and mimeographed the weekly church bulletin, besides teaching a women's Bible class in the Sunday school, and preparing our living room as a meeting place for a Sunday school class of young adults.

However, when my husband was called to another church, we felt it was only fair to submit the question of my continuing to work to the church board for an expression of their feelings on the matter. They informed us that they preferred that the pastor's wife not work. I guess they felt that if she worked it would convey an impression to the community that the church was not adequately supporting its minister and family. This church was very generous in their provisions for us, granting an adequate salary, a parsonage, utilities, a car allowance, and an amount designated for the minister's retirement fund.

By that time I had been promoted to a position of greater responsibility in the firm where I was employed and had just received a substantial increase in salary. I enjoyed the work, and it was good for my morale, in my early forties, to know that my return to the business world was accompanied with success. It bolstered my self-esteem to receive compliments on the quality of my work performance and the salary increases my superiors felt my work merited. However, since I considered my husband's work more important than mine, and since I valued a favorable attitude of the church toward him and me, I resigned my position.

I never regretted this decision. I really enjoyed the women's meetings in that church, teaching a women's Bible class, leading a Pioneer Girls Pilgrim group for three years, participating in the vacation Bible school, sponsoring the college-age group along with my husband, accompanying him as he visited members of our congregation. I also enjoyed the lovely spacious parsonage which was situated on a deep lot with tall trees front and back.

That pastorate was my husband's last pastorate, for while he was minister of that church he became ill with a malignancy, cancer of the marrow, which affected his blood and weakened his bone structure. When his ailment was diagnosed, the doctors told me he had a month to a year to live. However, he was a man of strong faith and determination and, in God's providence, he lived two years and seven months. As I look back on that period of time, I realize I couldn't have been with a group of Christians who would be more kind, thoughtful and generous than were the members of that church. There was one period of three months when he was confined to our home in a hospital bed or wheelchair because of a spinal ailment related to his illness. But the Lord gave a measure of restoration and he preached each Sunday for six months—until a month before his death. While he was limited in some of his activities, his pulpit ministry was powerful. A dedicated Christian man can't go through such experiences as he did without coming to know God better and looking at life from the perspective of one who knows he doesn't have long to serve God. One woman in our congregation commented, "When he was in the pulpit, you forgot he was a sick man."

So you can see why I am glad that I gave up my position and devoted myself completely to the work of the church and was able to spend more time with my husband during the six years of his last pastorate than would have been possible if I had continued to work.

3. A desire to escape the demands frequently made upon a minister's wife. When she's away from home all day, she doesn't have to answer the phone, go calling with her husband, or attend daytime meetings, some of which may bore her.

Yes, some ministers' wives are bored with the women's activities of the church. One such wife said, "The women's group at our church is composed of petty and superficial women who want me to participate in every activity, who pry into my life." One pastor's wife of whom I read was described as an intellectual woman who just couldn't adjust to the conversation of the wives of farmers who made up a large percentage of their church membership. She wasn't interested in their talk about their gardens, canning, the livestock on the farm, and so on. (I personally feel that you can discipline yourself to listen carefully to persons who have interests which are far different than yours. You can ask questions and thus enlarge your knowledge. As you show your interest in a person's work you give him a sense of value as a person, for each person's work is an important extension of his personality.)

Going to work may represent for a pastor's wife a way of dealing with her resentments, that is, her reactions to her husband's low salary and the expectations of the congregation. She may feel that the church members expect too much of her or that they want to get two persons for the price of one!

4. A compulsion for an outlet for talents and interests. Outside employment may represent for the minister's wife an opportunity to continue using the skills she learned while training for her career before marriage.

5. New opportunities to witness to persons with whom she might otherwise have little or no contact. One woman who was teaching school at the time I talked with her told me that the members of their congregation were proud of her involvement in this activity that touches families outside their church through her contact with children and other teachers and with parents through conferences and the PTA meetings.

I do not wish to pass judgment on those women who decide to work outside their homes, but it is my personal opinion that in most instances it would be better if the minister's wife did not seek outside employment. If she is employed, she cannot share as fully in the life of the church and in certain ministries of her husband. She will not have much time for intensive Bible study and prayer that will contribute to a rich spiritual ministry of her own. Nor will she have time for the people of their church families as persons, which is so important in counseling Christians and in winning individuals to faith in Jesus Christ as Saviour.

She needs to exercise discernment in making value judgments as she considers whether she should accept employment. A good prayer at such a time would be this: "Lord, help me ever to keep eternity's values in view."

25

Questions Asked by Pastors' Wives

Questions asked by pastors' wives get down to the nitty-gritty of their lives. For this reason I share some questions they have submitted to me—and my answers.

A woman in Ohio wrote: "I am a relatively young pastor's wife, and I would like to hear your point of view on do's and don'ts for a pastor's wife. For instance, just how far should we stretch ourselves with regard to serving in the church and attending meetings with small children in tow? And what about entertaining? I always feel reluctant to accept invitations to dinner because we can't afford to return the invitations as we would like to. These are just a few of my problems, but I must close now to get ready for children's Bible club here at our house."

Earlier in this book I referred to the conflict represented by this woman's first question—a conflict of responsibilities. All her life long she may be torn by such conflict. Her husband is not thus torn. Having dedicated his life to the preaching of the gospel, he usually puts his work ahead of his responsibility to his wife. A minister's wife, when first married, usually feels that her first responsibility is to her husband and his profession. But after children are born into their family, what then?

What about the wives of men in other professions? Let's think of the woman who is married to a doctor. He puts his work ahead of his family, but his wife isn't expected to serve his clients like the wife of a minister serves the people of her

155

husband's church. And the doctor's children aren't the objects of attention of his patients in the same way as children of a minister are noticed by members of their father's congregation. Futhermore, a doctor's family doesn't usually encounter the financial problems which face a minister and his family. Such financial problems mean that the pastor's wife needs to devote extra time and effort to her homemaking responsibilities because their economic situation requires this.

I may be giving the impression that I feel sorry for the woman who has to fill the role of pastor's wife, but I don't feel sorry for her. Rather, I am realistic about her problems. So often a pastor's wife doesn't have anyone with whom she can talk about her problems. Perhaps none of her own family live nearby, and she doesn't feel she can talk to members of their congregation about her problems. One minister's wife said she was longing for someone to call on her and let her tell them *her* troubles, but she had to pretend she didn't have any!

My correspondent's first question, "Just how far should we stretch ourselves with regard to serving in the church and attending meetings with small children in tow?" elicited this reply, "Only *you* can make that decision."

I think what troubles most ministers' wives in this area is their fear of what some of the congregation may say if the minister's wife isn't present at all meetings. However, you can't let such a fear control your decisions. You must do what is best for your children; they grow up only once.

On some occasions you will decide to hire a baby-sitter. If the expense of paying baby-sitters is a problem, perhaps you can contact some understanding woman in the church who will find teenage girls and others in your congregation whom she feels will be glad to baby-sit with your children when you attend women's meetings or go calling with your husband. Perhaps a committee could be formed to procure volunteer baby-sitters whose services could be rotated.

There may be times when you will decide to stay home with your children in order to give them more of your time and attention. Now that my children are grown, I wish I had spent more time with them when they were small. So now I advise young wives of ministers, "Be sure to spend enough time with your children."

I have already discussed the question of entertaining, but I will comment on this woman's specific problem of reluctance to accept invitations because she and her husband can't afford to reciprocate hospitality as they would like to. In my opinion, a minister's wife should not feel obligated to entertain in her home at dinner all those who have entertained her and her husband—and perhaps their children—at their home. I found that the people of our churches did not expect such reciprocity in entertaining. They were grateful that we were able to spare the time to be with them in their home for dinner and the good fellowship Christians enjoy when they converse with others about shared interests.

Since my correspondent asked that I give some dos and don'ts for pastors' wives, I include here some questions which came to me during a question-and-answer period after I had spoken at a Bible conference session for ministers' wives.

1. *Should a pastor's wife be expected to pinch-hit when asked at the last minute? Examples: teach Sunday school, chair a meeting, entertain.*

I would not object. Since I began filling the role of a pastor's wife with a good background in Bible study, I did not find it too difficult to pinch-hit for a Sunday school teacher.

If you are called on to teach a class of youngsters old enough to read, or adults, you could follow the method of asking all to read the lesson text for themselves. Then request each one to ask a question about the text. These could be questions of fact, of interpretation, or of application to an individual's life.

If you are unexpectedly asked to chair a meeting, this can

be done quite easily without preparation. If you are familiar with the regular order of business (reading of the minutes of the last meeting, treasurer's report, various committee reports, the taking up of old business and consideration of new business), you will find that things will not get too "messed up" just because you have been asked at the last minute. An advantage of not knowing ahead of time is that you don't have time to get nervous in anticipation of the meeting.

If someone who had planned to entertain a group suddenly becomes ill or is called out of town because of illness of a family member, or a death, and you are asked to open your home to the group, do so with warmhearted hospitality.

At one time Margaret Johnston Hess thought she couldn't entertain without cleaning venetian blinds, washing curtains, waxing floors, polishing furniture, scouring the brass, and polishing the silver. In an article which appeared in *Eternity* magazine in February, 1970, she told how her minister husband rebuked her on an occasion when she was reluctant to have the callers' meeting at the parsonage. He said, "Really, why do you make it so much work?"

She replied, "Well, you have to, don't you? You know how they do in this community. I don't go through half of what some of the others do—"

His black eyes flashed. "But that isn't hospitality—that's selfish pride. You don't have to do all that for the people who are coming—you're doing it for yourself—for your own selfish pride."

She winced. "But Mrs. Hrajek. Look what her house always looks like."

"But you can't compete with her. Why try? You have four children and two Bible classes. She has one house and no children. Anyway, that's her interest, the thing she likes to do. Why don't you just do it the way you can do it—and not make such a big thing out of it?"

She said to herself, *All right. Selfish pride. Probably you're right. Anyway, I'll try it. Something is wrong with me, certainly, in my attitude toward entertaining.*

The day of the meeting arrived. She did a little baking, but accepted all offers of help that had come. A friend served the coffee. She put the children to bed, and relaxed. She restrained herself from rushing around the last minute taking off the inevitable little fingermarks. She said to herself, *I'm going to enjoy it and I'm not going to pretend that we don't have fingermarks on our furniture all the time.*

She and everyone else had a wonderful time. And as she and her husband discussed the meeting, she said to him, "I guess you were right. It's just selfish pride to work the way I used to over entertaining people."

"Oh," he said, "didn't you work as hard this time? The house looked the same to me."

She was jubilant; she had learned how to entertain. Now she could have dinner guests just by setting an extra place. There would be no more of those candlelight, crystal goblet, children-out-of-sight efforts for her. She could have missionaries and anybody that happened along overnight. She had learned at last that hospitality is not impressing people; it is sharing what you have and are with them.[1]

2. *Should the pastor's wife be known as Mrs. Smith or Elizabeth?*

In my opinion, she should be spoken of as Mrs. Smith and addressed that way unless she herself asks to be addressed by her first name. She might like those in her own age bracket to call her by her first name.

3. *Should your husband let you know when he is bringing people home for dinner?*

Yes, if at all possible. But if someone should drop by to visit him at his study at the church and he decides on the spur of the moment to bring this person home to share lunch or supper at your home, take it in stride. Adopt the attitude of Margaret Johnston Hess: Hospitality is not impressing people; it is sharing what you have and are with them. Of course, your husband could phone you from the church study before he brings his visitors to the parsonage and thus give you a few minutes to prepare. And he could ask, "Is there anything you need from the store?" and pick it up for you on his way home.

4. *Should a wife go on visitation calls with her husband all the time or some of the time?*

If he wants her to accompany him on all calls and she wants to and is free, fine. But most wives don't go with their husbands on every call. Instead, they are selective. I nearly always accompanied my husband when he called on mothers of new babies, and usually on calls to homes where the family had been bereaved of a loved one.

5. *What is the degree of counseling which should be given when you recognize that professional help is needed?*

That counselor is wise who can sense his own limitations and direct the disturbed person to professional help. Many persons need someone to listen to them and are helped just by being able to talk with the minister or his wife about problems. They are given courage to go on as biblical principles are applied to the problem, followed by prayer together and assurance that the pastor and/or his wife will continue to pray about the counselee and his problems.

6. *What would you advise in a case where you are trying to help someone in need who demands a lot of your time, which in turn makes some of the other women in the church jealous?*

The persons I pity most in such a situation are those who become jealous because you spend a great deal of time with a woman who has a special need. In family situations, parents give more time to a sick child, to the one who has greater needs, than to those who are healthy and well adjusted.

The kind of jealousy to which you refer represents a selfish attitude and indicates a lack of spiritual maturity. I don't know of any other way to deal with it but to tell such a person, "The fact that I spend so much time with this person doesn't mean that I love you less. It's just that her needs are greater than yours."

You can make your brief contacts with these jealous individuals meaningful by displaying your very personal interest in them.

7. *What should we do about a woman with a mental problem which seems to be caused by her going through the menopause?*

First, I would urge her to see her doctor if she hasn't already done so. He can prescribe medication that will alleviate some of the distressing symptoms.

Next, encourage her to take a positive attitude toward those symptoms; that is, urge her to minimize them instead of magnifying them. Too many women are influenced by old wives' tales about the menopause.

A woman who at this period in her life is depressed and tired, perhaps irritable at times, and cries easily, is giving evidence that she cannot handle life's problems as well as she used to; every molehill seems like a mountain.

Exercise patience with this woman, but if she takes up too much of your time, let her know (with firmness and graciousness) that other individuals need you too. You can't let one person monopolize your time to the neglect of your husband, your children, and other persons in your congregation.

8. *Should a pastor take a day off?*

Yes. He will do better work during six days for having taken one day for rest and recreation. Of course, he could take two half days instead of one full day if such an arrangement works out better for him and his work.

9. *Should a pastor and his wife have close friends in their congregation?*

A pastor's wife from the state of Iowa who wrote to me in response to one of my radio programs said, "Today you talked about the value of a real friend in whom one can freely confide. Having such a friend is an experience that I feel has been denied me in almost twenty-eight years as a pastor's wife. I am nearly always 'on guard.' How have you handled this delicate problem in your experience?"

I think many pastors' wives start out in their husbands' first pastorate feeling like they're walking on eggs. They're on guard because they have heard so much about jealousy and envy if the pastor and his wife relate more closely to some members of their congregation than they do to others.

It's part of our humanity that we want close friends, friends who are loyal, friends in whom we have confidence and in whom, therefore, we can confide. In my experience I found it best to develop such friendships outside of the congregation which my husband was pastoring. We tried to treat all members of the congregation alike, though I must admit it wasn't easy, for some people attract you more than others, are more outgoing, and want to do things for you which express their affection. But you must be alert to the possibility of acquiring a sense of obligation to anyone because of his gifts which may lead you or your husband to feel you need to give to this person or his family members special consideration in church activities.

Try to find another couple (even if they live twenty-five or thirty miles away) with whom you can get together frequently, or a couple in your town from another church.

It may be part of the price of serving God effectively to have to do without the close friendships for which you long, but God is able to give you other compensations. I have found this true. One of the compensations is this: You have a closer relationship with your husband and his work than do other wives. And when you come to a new location you are automatically provided with a group of people who are interested in you and want to know you, and who will show you many kindnesses, even though you may not allow yourself to get involved in close friendships with them, the kind in which you can "let down your hair." So, be thankful for these blessings.

10. *What do you do when lay leadership is lacking?*

More than a year ago I received a letter from a pastor's wife in a town with a population of about five thousand. Her husband is pastor of a church in an area which she described as "sort of an urban-rural area." In her letter she said, "Many times we have become discouraged in our work. It seems right now we are at a plateau. We have been here eight years. When we first came here, the building in which we worshipped was a two-story frame house. After a year we moved to a government building where we met for two years, and then we began worshipping in our new church building. Later we added an educational wing. We are thankful for these new buildings, but we recognize that it takes more than a building to carry on the Lord's work.

"I wonder if you found in your ministry that most of the work (among the lay people) is done by just the same few and that they get tired of always being asked to serve?"

This varies from church to church. Some churches have a predominance of older people who may become tired, and have feelings like the church member who said to me, "Well, we worked hard during the years when the church was getting started and while it was being built up. We're tired; let the younger folk take over now."

I really admire the young couples I have observed who, though they have several small children, enthusiastically engage in various church activities. For some, these church activities represent their social life, for they center their social life in the church. But often these couples are individuals who have a good education (the wife is a teacher or nurse and the husband has leadership talents), and they don't want to wait until their children are grown before putting their talents to work in the Lord's service. Working in the church gives another dimension to their life together, and it gives their growing children an example of parents who think enough of their church to put something of themselves into it.

I heard the pastor of one church say that the church was sadly lacking in leadership, for practically all of its male members were blue-collar workers. No one should assume that men whose jobs are described as "blue-collar jobs" wouldn't be capable of leadership in a church, but in the opinion of the pastor, leadership potential among the men of this particular church was definitely lacking.

In my opinion, one of the important ministries of a pastor and his wife is that of developing lay leadership. For this reason it is best for a minister's wife not to hold office in the women's organizations of the church. However, she can be a resource person to whom women can come for advice, suggestions, and materials for special programs. She can be on the lookout for material that she comes across in magazines, books, and other sources, that will fit into the themes of New Year's, Lent, Easter, Mother's Day, Thanksgiving, and Christmas. She might even encourage members of the women's society to collect such material and place it in a file at the church. As new program committees are appointed each year, they should be informed that this file is available for their use.

11. *What about lack of courtesy?*

The same pastor's wife wrote, "We have tried Pastor's Night when our council members invite some of the church members for coffee and cookies, and then my husband visits and talks with them.

"The thing that surprises me these days is the lack of manners people have shown in failing to call us if they aren't able to come to these sessions. They are invited by phone and usually checked on later.

"Yesterday we had open house in our home for the sixteen members of our church board and their wives. Four had indicated they would be unable to attend, seven were present with their wives, but no word was received from the other five. Is this a common thing—just not showing up and failing to call, or are these people so busy with other things that they forget? I do realize that things come up or unexpected company puts in an appearance, but they could pick up the telephone to let us know they won't be able to come.

"Maybe their bringing-up was different from mine. I was brought up to write thank-you notes, and so on. In fact, my mother, who lives twenty miles from us, still reminds me to write notes of thanks."

In answer to the question about the lack of courtesy on the part of those persons who are invited to the pastor's home for a social occasion, I can only say this: You observe this lack of courtesy and consideration and feel sad about it, but there's nothing you can do about it. In spite of the failings of church members, the pastor and his wife must present a cheerful, courteous facade and not wear their feelings on their sleeves.

We are not responsible for how people act toward us, but we *are* responsible for how we act toward others. Let all that you do be done in love, for love cannot be wasted. Even though for a time it seems that your love brings no repsonse, I would urge you to be patient and be confident that you will be most blessed when you *give* love, with no thought of its being returned.

12. *What does a preacher's wife say when someone comments on her husband's sermon? Something like "Oh, it really wasn't anything"?*

No. It would be better to say something like this: "I thought it was wonderful, too, but then I always think so. I'm prejudiced." Or, if you couldn't honestly say that, you could simply say, "I'm glad you enjoyed his sermon."

13. *Should a wife pass on to her minister-husband criticisms given to her by members of the congregation?*

No. She might say to one who evidently expects her to pass

on criticisms, "Why don't you go to him directly?" or "Why don't you speak to a member of the board about that?"

Be realistic and face the fact that no one can be in a public position without being criticized. A minister can't please everybody. A couple in a pastorate should keep in mind that they should aim, first and foremost, to please God. However, adopting such an attitude does not necessarily mean you will be inconsiderate of the feelings of people.

I have always been irked by the criticism implied when someone calls at nine o'clock in the morning and asks, "Oh, did I get you out of bed?" So many parishioners think the minister's job (and his wife's) is a snap, and do not realize how much time is required to study, to pray about all phases of the work of the church, and to supervise those who assist him in handling details.

If a minister refuses to be an errand boy for the church, some will criticize. And if he is the kind of person who just cannot refuse those persons who thoughtlessly take advantage of him, he is criticized for being "an easy mark" and not devoting his time to things of greater importance.

It's difficult for the minister's wife to know that her husband is being criticized by members of the congregation. Not all ministers are eminently successful. When people point up your husband's failures, you want to do something. You may find yourself tempted to lash out at those who seem to be threatening your husband. But you are too closely identified with your husband to become involved. Your most effective help will be given by remaining quietly loving and affectionate, being a good listener when he needs a sounding board, and praying with him and for him.

14. *Should a wife ever express to her husband criticism of his sermons?*

Not if she is aware that he is extremely sensitive to criticism. I read somewhere a suggestion for the wife of a man who is sensitive to criticism. When he asks his wife for an evaluation of his sermon she "might limit her comments to favorable ones. She can give praise, even if she only praises his diction."

However, I feel that we need to be careful about offering only praise. Someone has said, "Praise for the sake of praise can become an insult to a man of integrity."

Honesty is essential in the relationship between a minister and his wife as in any husband-wife relationship. However, sometimes we can be ruthlessly honest with an intent to hurt. If a woman finds herself criticizing her husband, she had better examine her motives for criticizing. Her criticism might be just an outlet for her frustrations, with her husband as the whipping boy.

15. *Should a woman ever help her husband with his sermon?*

Sermon preparation isn't a group project. The sermon should represent the outpouring of the heart of a man to whom God has spoken. Of course, at times when a man is under a great deal of pressure because of numerous demands on his time, he might ask his wife to do some research for him, if she is capable of doing so. After all, many men in business and government, as well as pastors of large churches, have a staff on whom they can call for such assistance. If the minister's wife is able to do something like this for him, she will be learning and will be sharing in his ministry, as well as contributing to their person-to-person relationship through this kind of sharing.

I have heard of some men who are good pastors but are not good preachers. The wife of a man who cannot preach well must endure this inadequacy of her husband with courage and love, and she may suffer very much. But, like the members of the church, she will need to put over against this inadequacy his talents in relating to individuals, in empathizing with them in their sorrows, griefs, trials, and so on.

I visited in the home of a minister and his wife until past

midnight on an occasion when I was an overnight guest in their home after speaking to the women and girls of their church at a banquet. I was delighted to observe the rapport between these two. He happily volunteered the information that his wife was an "idea woman" as far as projects in the church were concerned, that she was a good organizer, and that he was the one who implemented the plans and worked out the details. Instead of competing, this husband and wife beautifully complemented each other.

Epilogue

As you have walked with me through the chapters of this book, we have talked not only about the problems of a minister's wife but also about the privileges.

One of the major privileges is that you are part of a "team" that is bringing the gospel of God's offer of forgiveness and His promise of new life to those who believe in His Son, Jesus Christ. You are part of a team that is bringing the Word of God to bear upon the lives of people to transform them, to enable them to live more meaningful, stable, and helpful lives. You and your husband are teammates, not competitors.

Eugenia Price in her book *A Woman's Choice* referred to a competitive relationship between a minister and his wife in the area of counseling. She said:

> Someone told . . . of having called the home of a local minister, hoping to talk for a few minutes about a problem with the minister's wife, who had a reputation as a counselor with women. The minister answered the telephone, since his wife was not at home. Would he have a spare moment to advise this woman?
>
> "No, ma'am, not on your life!" he replied curtly. "My wife's the advice-giver around here. I stay strictly out of her territory!"
>
> The woman who wanted advice, wisely did not call back. She sensed the unhealthy *competition* between this man and woman and went to another source.[1]

Such competition can nibble at the marriage relationship like a horde of energetic termites; if not seen for what it is and

169

honestly dealt with, it will hamper the effectiveness of the minister and his wife.

When a husband and wife come to recognize the existence of such a competitive spirit as a barrier to harmony in their relationship and as an attitude which grieves the Holy Spirit, they must confess to God their need of His power to enable them to change their attitudes. They can also rely on the Holy Spirit to lead them into understanding cooperation instead of competition as they serve their Lord.

Even though you view yourselves as teammates, this does not mean that your husband should not take the position of leadership, for every team needs a captain. Your husband should lead in working out a relationship in which you and he agree on your aims. You have to agree on your aims, or you will not succeed. "Agreeing to agree" does not mean that your personality will be submerged. If your husband is wise, he will allow you to be who you are; and you, of course, should let him be who he is.

The team concept should also apply to the bringing up of your children. Both husband and wife should be involved in this project. Many a pastor's wife feels that too much of the responsibility for the children is left up to her, and her burden is increased if she feels that the normal problems of family life are magnified because of the "fishbowl existence" of their family.

However, ministers, as well as their wives, can feel tension on this account. I heard Dr. Henry Brandt, Christian psychologist, say at a conference session for pastors and their wives that great tensions may develop if the husband feels that their family must be a model of Christian living if he is to be effective as a pastor. It's true that pastors and their families are highly visible. Dr. Brandt suggested that the pastor and his wife, instead of considering this visibility as a burden, take this view: "We have an opportunity to give leadership to the families of our congregation by way of example."

You should be putting into practice the principles for family living found in Ephesians 5:21—6:4 and Colossians 3:13-21, as well as the principles of right living for individuals found throughout the New Testament. You will want to measure your love for one another by the description of love found in 1 Corinthians 13 and other passages in the New Testament. The husband has an especially large assignment when he is told to love his wife *as* Christ loved the church. This requires self-sacrificial love and a desire for his wife's physical, emotional, and spiritual well-being.

A wife will not find it difficult to submit to a husband who loves her in that way. In my opinion, a woman should not think of submission as servitude, as so many do. Servitude is what is seen in the relationship of a slave to a master, a relationship which is often referred to in the Bible. I like the way some contemporary versions of the New Testament render passages about a wife's submission to her husband. They indicate that she should adapt herself to her husband and fit in with his plans.

If marriage partners accept the definition of love that states that "love is that which seeks the highest good of the one loved," and make that kind of love their mutual aim, much friction will be eliminated from family living. Self-seeking and wanting one's own way will be judged as unworthy attitudes. If a man loves his wife with *agape* love (God's kind of love), he will not neglect his wife or his children. And their response to his showing them his love by giving them his time and attention will in all likelihood be expressed in a consideration for his needs and a desire to avoid bringing reproach upon his ministry.

In that connection, I cannot help but recall something my youngest son told me during his college years. He said, "Mother, when I was in high school, there were some things I *wanted* to do but didn't do, for the sake of Dad's ministry."

As I view your life as a pastor's wife, I am convinced that

no life is more challenging and none offers greater opportunities for helping others. You have a great variety of activities, and as you engage in these activities you will develop as a person.

Your life can be summed up in relationships—relationships which involve you as a person with other persons. First and foremost is your relationship with God. Be sure to nurture this relationship through daily contact with Him by spending time with His message to man, the Bible, and by communing with Him in prayer.

You should also nurture other relationships—with your husband, your children, the people of your church, and the people of your community (as time and strength allow, and as the Lord leads you).

You may be asking a question similar to that found in 2 Corinthians 2:16: "Who is sufficient for these things?" Or, "Who is qualified for it [this ministry]?" as the Berkeley Version (v. 17) translates. Or: "Who could think himself adequate for a responsibility like this?" as J. B. Phillips translates.

The answer to this question is found in 2 Corinthians 3:6: "Our sufficiency is of God." He has qualified us; He will make us adequate for our responsibilities.

The Lord Jesus will enable you, qualify you, and make you competent for that service to which He has called you. You can be as sure of this as was the apostle Paul when he wrote, "I can do all things through Him [Christ] who strengthens me" (Phil 4:13, NASB). Of course the words "all things" refer to all things that the Lord wants you to do. If God hasn't given you musical aptitudes, don't expect that He will enable you to play like Van Cliburn.

I like the rendering of Philippians 4:13, the verse I have just quoted, as found in the Amplified Version: "I have strength for all things in Christ Who empowers me—I am ready for anything and equal to anything through Him Who infuses inner strength into me, [that is, I am self-sufficient in Christ's sufficiency]."

Thank God day by day for this sufficiency, reckon on it, and you will find life as a pastor's wife to be one of "joy in serving Jesus."

Notes

Chapter 2
1. Editorial, *Pastoral Psychology,* Dec. 1961, p. 9.
2. From *The Role of the Minister's Wife,* by Wallace Denton, The Westminster Press. Copyright © MCMLXII, W. L. Jenkins. Used by permission.
3. Ibid., p. 27.
4. Ibid., p. 29.
5. Ibid., p. 28.
6. Ibid., p. 32.

Chapter 4
1. William G. T. Douglas, *Ministers' Wives* (New York: Harper & Row, 1965).
2. Douglas, "Ministers Wives: Problems and Resources," *Seminary Quarterly,* Winter 1966, published by Ministers Life and Casualty Union, Minneapolis, Minn., p. 3. Reprinted from *Christian Advocate,* Nov. 18, 1965. Copyright 1965 by the Methodist Publishing House.
3. Ibid.
4. Anna B. Mow, *Your Child* (Grand Rapids: Zondervan, 1963), pp. 25-26.

Chapter 6
1. Marian Van Dam, "Pastor's Wife," *Moody Monthly* 64, no. 2 (Oct. 1963): 44. Reprinted from Moody Monthly. Used by permission. Copyright 1963 by The Moody Bible Institute of Chicago.
2. Wallace Denton, *The Role of the Minister's Wife* (Philadelphia: Westminster, 1951), p. 27.
3. William Whyte, Jr., "The Wives of Management," *Fortune* 44 (Oct. 1951): 86. Reprinted from the October 1951 issue of Fortune Magazine by special permission; © 1951 Time Inc.
4. *Moody Monthly* 61, no. 5 (Jan. 1961): 51. Reprinted from Moody Monthly. Used by permission. Copyright 1961 by The Moody Bible Institute of Chicago.

Chapter 8
1. Jhan and June Robbins, "What Ministers Hate Most About the Ministry," *This Week* magazine, Aug. 20, 1961, pp. 6-7.
2. "Why I *Like* the Ministry," *This Week* magazine, Oct. 22, 1961.

Chapter 9
1. Dorothy Thompson, "I'm the Child of a King," *Ladies' Home Journal,* Nov. 1949, p. 11 ff. © 1959 Downe Publishing, Inc. Reprinted by Special Permission of the Ladies' Home Journal.

Chapter 10
1. Kenneth S. Wuest, *Hebrews in the Greek New Testament for the English Reader* (Grand Rapids: Eerdmans, 1948), p. 234. Used by permission.
2. Ibid.

3. F. F. Bruce, *The Letters of Paul*, American ed. (Grand Rapids: Eerdmans, 1965), p. 93. Copyright 1965, Paternoster Press, Exeter, Devon, England. Used by permission.
4. "Practical Problems of Ministers: A 'Follow-up Report," published by Ministers Life and Casualty Union, Minneapolis, Minn., Aug. 1967.
5. Bruce, p. 175.

Chapter 11
1. Cecil G. Osborne, *The Art of Understanding Your Mate* (Grand Rapids: Zondervan, 1970), pp. 23-26.
2. Marion H. Nelson, *Why Christians Crack Up!* Rev. ed. (Chicago: Moody, 1967), pp. 56-59.
3. George Sweeting, *And the Greatest of These* (Westwood, N. J.: Revell, 1968) p. 24. Used by permission of the Fleming H. Revell Co.

Chapter 12
1. Kenneth S. Wuest, *Wuest's Expanded Translation of the Greek New Testament*, vol. 3 (Grand Rapids: Eerdmans, 1959), p. 125. Used by permission.
2. Gladys and Gordon DePree, *A Blade of Grass* (Grand Rapids: Zondervan, 1967), p. 46.

Chapter 13
1. Ted W. Engstrom and Alec Mackenzie, *Managing Your Time* (Grand Rapids: Zondervan, 1967), pp. 26-29.
2. Ibid., pp. 29-30.

Chapter 16
1. Joseph T. Bayly, "Out of My Mind," *Eternity* 13, no. 12 (Dec. 1962): 33.
2. Edna Gerstner, *Idelette* (Grand Rapids: Zondervan, 1963), pp. 71-72. Used by permission.

Chapter 17
1. Cecil G. Osborne, *The Art of Understanding Your Mate* (Grand Rapids: Zondervan, 1970) p. 25.
2. Ibid., p. 23.
3. Carolyn P. Blackwood, *The Pastor's Wife* (Philadelphia: Westminster, 1951), p. 30.

Chapter 18
1. Eugenia Price, *A Woman's Choice* (Grand Rapids: Zondervan, 1962), p. 116.
2. Alton Blakeslee and Jeremiah Stamler, *Your Heart Has Nine Lives*, 4th ed. (New York: Simon & Schuster, Pocket Books, 1967).
3. Ardis Whitman, "What Makes a Woman Unforgettable?" *Woman's Day*, Oct. 1962, pp. 45, 200.
4. Ibid., pp. 100-103.
5. Ibid., p. 103.

Chapter 19
1. Wallace Denton, *The Role of the Minister's Wife* (Philadelphia: Westminster, 1951), p. 27.
2. Ibid., p. 63.
3. Ibid., p. 67.
4. Ibid., pp. 67-68.

Chapter 20
1. Dorothy Pentecost, *The Pastor's Wife and the Church* (Chicago: Moody, 1964).
2. Eugenia Price, *Make Love Your Aim* (Grand Rapids: Zondervan, 1967), pp. 37-38.

Chapter 21
1. From *Bless This Mess and Other Prayers* by Jo Carr and Imogene Sorley, p. 105. Copyright © 1969 by Abingdon Press.

Chapter 22
1. Cecil G. Osborne, *The Art of Understanding Your Mate* (Grand Rapids: Zondervan, 1970), p. 77.

Chapter 25
1. Margaret Johnston Hess, "Hospitality or Pride?" *Eternity* 21, no. 2, (Feb. 1970): 13, 19.

Epilogue
1. Eugenia Price. *A Woman's Choice* (Grand Rapids: Zondervan, 1962), p. 87.